SONNET FOR A WRITER FRIEND

(for Ed)

The story was a good one, not your best,
I think, but with a certain crisp elan.
"I don't mind pain," your character confessed.
"I wouldn't say that to just any man."
You hadn't asked permission. Did I care?
And, anyway, who owns the spoken word?
My first reaction was that you had dared
To make our playful passion seem absurd.
But now I've come to treasure tangled things—
A skein of jazz; a variegated riff
Of family; the chaos prayer brings;
The way a friendship braids into a life;
The curse and blessing of a writer. And
I wouldn't say that to just any man.

MELANIE TEM'S
FRY DAY
PLAYS & POEMS

BY MELANIE TEM

CROSSROAD PRESS

INTRODUCTION

STEVE RASNIC TEM

Melanie is probably best known for the nine horror novels she published in the nineties with Dell Abyss, Headline UK, and The Women's Press, along with ninety plus fantasy and horror short stories. What readers outside Colorado may not know is that she devoted much of her creative energy the last fifteen years of her life to other forms: Poetry, plays, and oral storytelling.

As a child Melanie loved poetry and with her father's encouragement memorized a large number of poems which she would recite for him in the evenings (she was allowed to watch very little TV). From time to time she also wrote poetry, but not seriously until—approaching her fiftieth birthday—she felt the urge to write a cycle of poems in celebration. The best of those poems—about her friends, life with me and our children, and other domestic observations—are included here, along with some genre-related poetry that editors Tom Piccirilli and Al Sarrantonio encouraged her to write.

About the same time as this resurgent interest in poetry, Melanie fell in love with live performance, and oral storytelling in particular. What fascinated her about the art form was the intimate and dynamic connection storytellers can develop with their audience, along with the excitement of creating and recreating a story on the spot, incorporating the emotional timbre and feedback of the moment. She attended workshops and conferences in the art form and incorporated the techniques she learned into her own creative work. Melanie performed stories at a variety of venues over the years. By nature, storytelling is a somewhat ephemeral art form, and she never wrote any of these pieces down, but I talked her into letting me record four of them. You can download/listen to them at https://m-s-tem.band-camp.com/releases: Four tales about poetry, 'possums, a really big misunderstanding, and a really big hat.

Melanie's experiences with storytelling sparked a renewed passion for plays as a creative outlet. Our first few dates were largely spent going to plays together, beginning with David Mamet's *American Buffalo,* and over the years we must have seen hundreds. At a certain point she became obsessed with plays, reading and studying them, taking them apart to see how they worked. She joined Colorado Dramatists and began writing plays of her own.

I believe some of Melanie's best writing occurs in her plays. They are about some of the same subjects which imbued her fiction—primarily the horrors which haunt families, grief, and profound loss—but elevated through the use of theatrical presentation. They also reach beyond the dramas affecting a particular family to address such topics as capital punishment and the potential danger of rebirthing therapy.

Melanie's play *Fry Day* incorporates characters, themes, and language from two of her short stories, "Fry Day," and "Lightning Rod," to create a dramatic whole even greater than its parts. If interested, you can read these stories in her massive career-defining collection *Singularity and Other Stories* (Crossroad Press).

Comfort Me with Peaches was inspired by the diaries of Roberta Robertson, a friend she met in a bereavement group after the death of our son Anthony. Roberta was a remarkable person, a nurse for many decades who had kept a daily journal since 1938. She also lost two children, including one who was an apparent victim of serial killer Ted Bundy.

Steve Rasnic Tem
May 2020

Note: Any group interested in performing one of Melanie's plays should contact me through my website contact form: http://stevetem.com/contact/.

ACKNOWLEDGMENTS

"Samhain" originally appeared in *Halloween: New Poems* ed. by Al Sarrantonio, Cemetery Dance, 2010.

The following poems originally appeared in The Devil's Wine ed. by Tom Piccirilli, Cemetery Dance, 2004: "Primordial Haiku," "Uncommon Name," "The Day I Rode Go-Carts with My Son," "Taking Nourishment," "Dinner Conversations," "Certain Light," "Cacodemon," "Woman Wailing," "Silent Letter," "Seeing You Whole."

Performance information for each play is included in the Production History.

CONTENTS

PLAYS

POEMS –191

PLAYS

THE SOCIETY FOR LOST POSITIVES

POSITIVES

A PLAY IN ONE ACT

Production History

The Society for Lost Positives had its world premiere in 2001 at the Federal Theater in Denver, Colorado as part of the Colorado Dramatists One-Act Play Contest. In 2003 it was produced as part of the Stage Left Theatre One-Act Play Festival in Salida, Colorado. In 2004 it was performed at the Heartland Theatre in Chicago, Illinois.

Characters

MR. ST. CLARE, a retired high school English teacher, late seventies
CLAUDIA MALCOLM, his former student, late forties

Time and Place

The play takes place in present day, MR. ST. CLARE'S living room, once elegant but now unkempt. Dusty and cluttered antique furniture (loveseat, wingback chairs) stand on a plush, soiled white carpet. Dirty dishes litter tabletops. A flip chart facing the audience shows an ongoing list of lost positives, including those in MR. ST. CLARE's opening monologue as well as DAIN (from "disdain"), RISION (from "derision"), and GUST (from "disgust").

SCENE ONE

At rise, MR. ST. CLARE is standing by a flip chart as if in front of a classroom, cane in his hand which he uses as a pointer, several dictionaries on the desk beside him. He writes on the chart with a thick black marker so the words are visible to the audience, teaching students who aren't there, addressing them by name, pausing as if to hear their responses and questions, maintaining the strict discipline he was known for during his teaching career.

MR. ST. CLARE: This meeting of the Society for Lost Positives will now come to order. The first order of business is the payment of dues, which, as you know, is assessed at one lost positive per meeting. *(He indicates the chart.)*

A minimal requirement, surely not taxing to anyone's intellectual powers. Let us begin with— *(He pauses, keeping students in suspense.)*

—Mr. Merritt.

(Throughout the following monologue, he points at one empty chair after another as he announces the name of each imaginary student he's calling on to recite. With the cane/pointer he taps on the floor for emphasis, bangs the desk to get the attention of presumably distracted students, even raises it threateningly and advances as if to rap someone's head or knuckles. Each lost positive he writes with a flourish on the chart. His manner is by turns icy, mocking, and sternly approving.)

MR. Merritt. You *have* come prepared to pay the required dues, have you not? What's that? COUTH? Ah, yes, COUTH. A commodity in woefully short supply among some members of this august company. Next. Miss Watson. Miss Watson, we're waiting. EPT, yes. How appropriate. EPT. MR. Lemanski.

Three? You do understand there is no extra credit or payment in advance? EFFABLE, yes, from INEFFABLE. LETE. Ha! Very good! From DELETE. And? And COMBOBULATED from DISCOMBOBULATED. Now there's a positive we truly need to reclaim for use in this group. Next! Miss Valente! What's that? Speak up, Miss Valente, so we can all appreciate your erudition. FLOWERED, did you say? As in DEFLOWERED? It is a sad fact, class, that once there has been a *de*flowering the positive, the flowering, is indeed irretrievably lost. As Miss Valente well knows. Anyone else? *(He gestures, includes the audience.)*

Anyone else? Other lost positives to add to the list?

(The doorbell rings. He starts and frowns, goes on with his monologue in a slightly more urgent tone.)

The language, not to say the world, is replete with positives which, due to disuse, have been lost to the general populace. It is the mission here, at the Society for Lost Positives, to reclaim them from that oblivion. PLUSSED. DESCRIPT. CONSCIONABLE. IMICAL. EMBOWEL—which has much the same difficulty as FLOWERED, does it not, Miss Valente? ANTHROPY. OGYNY. IN SORTS. Not that I, mind you, am ever *mis*anthropic, *misogy*nistic, or *out of* sorts. Wouldn't you agree, Miss Valente? *(The doorbell rings again.)*

Isn't that right, MR. Oberon? Miss Watson? MR. Castarena? *(He raps his cane sternly on the desk.)*

Class! You are to ignore this *uncouth* attempt to intrude upon our proceedings. I can assure you that whoever it is has no business here, at *my* door, uninvited. *(He writes on the chart, a bit shakily.)*

CREANT!

(The doorbell rings again, loud and long, followed this time by pounding. Pause. Then MR. ST. CLARE makes his way to the door, muttering, moving laboriously, and unlocks several locks in order to open it a crack.)

Yes?

CLAUDIA *(offstage)*: MR. St. Clare?

MR. ST. CLARE: Whatever you are selling, or for whatever Worthy cause you are soliciting, I am not interested. *(He starts to shut the door, but she prevents him.)*

CLAUDIA: Can I come in?

MR. ST. CLARE: I am sure you *can,* but you *may* not.

(She pushes in past him, nearly knocking him off-balance, and comes to stand, hands on hips, surveying the room.)

MR. ST. CLARE: How dare you!

CLAUDIA: Oh, Chill.

MR. ST. CLARE: A total stranger—

CLAUDIA: We're not exactly strangers, MR. St. Clare.

MR. ST. CLARE: My dear, you are most definitely a stranger to me. And shall, I hope and trust, remain so.

CLAUDIA *(surveying the room)*: Somehow I knew you'd have a white carpet.

MR. ST. CLARE: Can I help you in some way?

CLAUDIA: Live alone, do you?

MR. ST. CLARE: I *beg* your pardon

CLAUDIA: Piss off your cleaning lady?

(He attempts to stack the strewn newspapers.)

MR. ST. CLARE: I will not have some strange woman—

(CLAUDIA goes to the chart of lost positives.)

CLAUDIA: What's this?

MR. ST. CLARE: I am quite sure you would find that of little interest—

CLAUDIA: Well, would you look at this. It's the Society for Lost Positives!

(He raises his cane to point at her in a gesture intended to be authoritative. But he loses his balance, almost drops the cane and flails for it.)

MR. ST. CLARE: And just who are you, pray tell?

CLAUDIA: You don't remember me? Why am I not surprised? Claudia Malcolm. I was in your sophomore English class.

MR. ST. CLARE: Good God, how many years ago?

CLAUDIA: Thirty-two. And counting.

MR. ST. CLARE: I have no memory of you whatsoever, I'm afraid, and no wish to rekindle our alleged acquaintance. Please leave my home.

CLAUDIA: Well, MR. St. Clare, I remember you.

MR. ST. CLARE: Of course.

CLAUDIA: Still the same old arrogant son-of-a-bitch, aren't you? Glad to see it. Still throwing dictionaries at people who aren't hanging on your every word? Still making fun of people till they're in tears if they don't know the answer to one of your dumb-ass questions?

MR. ST. CLARE: I have been retired from teaching for seventeen ye—

CLAUDIA: I guess you would be, wouldn't you. It's hard to think of you as anything but a teacher.

MR. ST. CLARE: Well, yes.

CLAUDIA: What do you *do* if you don't teach anymore? Aren't you bored?

MR. ST. CLARE: Those of us with intellectual interests and acumen are seldom bored.

CLAUDIA: Well aren't you special? DAIN. RISION. GUST. Definitely lost those positives, haven't you? If you ever had them in the first place.

MR. ST. CLARE: Is that why you're here, Miss—Markham, is it?

CLAUDIA: Malcolm. And it's Ms.

MR. ST. CLARE: To tell me how I hurt your feelings and bruised your self-esteem when you were in high school?

(*He gives her an exaggerated bow, then goes to the door, thumping his cane loudly to mark every step. He jerks the door open all the way and gestures imperiously.*)

Fine, then. Now you have unburdened yourself.

CLAUDIA: Not quite. (*She strides across the room, pulls the door out of his hand, shuts it and locks all the locks.*)

MR. ST. CLARE: Who do you think you are?

CLAUDIA: Shouldn't that be "whom"?

MR. ST. CLARE: Who.

CLAUDIA: You sure?

MR. ST. CLARE: Indeed.

CLAUDIA: I'm Claudia Malcolm. Former student. Dying woman. A thirty-two-year member of the Society for Lost Positives.

MR. ST. CLARE: You were never—

CLAUDIA: The one time, the one and only time, you ever

said anything nice to me was because I came up with a lost positive nobody else had thought of. For just a second there, you were impressed.

MR. ST. CLARE: I find that hard to believe.

CLAUDIA: You were shocked that somebody like me, not one of your pets, would even know a word like that. Do you remember what it was? *(She waits. When he doesn't answer, she shouts and punches her fists in the air, to his great disapproval.)*

EXORABLE! *(She waits again. He is not impressed.)*

EXORABLE. EVITABLE. As in something you *can* stop or avoid. Unlike death.

MR. ST. CLARE: EXORABLE is really rather common—

CLAUDIA: Hey, I spent a lot of time reading the damn dictionary to get that word. *Reading* the dictionary. I can't believe I actually did that. Just so I could join some stupid club that doesn't even really exist.

MR. ST. CLARE: You are not and never have been a member of the Society for Lost Positives. Our membership is quite select.

CLAUDIA: Fuck you.

(He is appalled. She rushes to the chart and writes EXORABLE on it in big block letters.)

EXORABLE! You hear me? EXORABLE! I paid my goddamn dues!

SCENE TWO

An hour or so later. MR. ST. CLARE sits rigidly on the loveseat, cane like a scepter in his hand. Attempts have been made to straighten up the room. CLAUDIA enters, lugging an upright vacuum cleaner. As she passes the chart, on which a few more lost positives have been added in both her sloppy, somewhat childish writing and his elegant script (e.g.: PERTURBABLE, CHOATE, IMITABLE, PERTINENT), she is struck by inspiration and stops to write HEVELED, CREPIT, KEMPT, and WIELDY. Then she pushes the unwieldy vacuum cleaner into the open space of white carpet and looks around for an outlet.

CLAUDIA: This'll have to be cleaned, but maybe I can get the loose stuff—

MR. ST. CLARE: I shall summon the police. I shall have you arrested.

CLAUDIA: For what? Vacuuming?

MR. ST. CLARE: Trespassing.

CLAUDIA: Well, let's see. I'm your favorite niece and you're a little senile and you don't always know who I am.

(They glare at each other for a long moment. Then she barks a sudden, loud laugh and writes GUISE.)

MR. ST. CLARE: Yes, yes, DISGUISE. I have always been rather fond of that one because it is an example of a positive twice lost. Which is to say: GUISE, the presumed positive of DISGUISE, is still in use in common parlance, but as a negative itself, as in "under the guise of"—

(She plugs in the vacuum cleaner, turns it on, grimaces at how loud it is. He turns away from the offensive noise, as though simply to banish it from his notice. She pushes the vacuum back and forth a few times, then gives up and turns it off.)

CLAUDIA: How long since you've used this thing?

MR. ST. CLARE: *I* have never used it.

(She crouches and, with effort and accompanying epithets, manages to open the vacuum cleaner and remove the bag, which is very full.)

CLAUDIA: I don't suppose you have any new bags.

MR. ST. CLARE: I'm sure I wouldn't know.

CLAUDIA: Your wife takes care of all the domestic shit, right? So you can—what? Think?

MR. ST. CLARE: My wife is deceased.

CLAUDIA *(pause)*: Lot of that going around. *(pause)* I met your wife a couple of times. Well, I *saw* her. It's not like you introduced me. Tall skinny blonde, voice like aluminum foil. No offense.

MR. ST. CLARE: I must say, that is quite a nice simile, Miss Malcolm.

CLAUDIA: Thanks. I'm sorry about your wife. Her name was Lois, wasn't it?

MR. ST. CLARE: My wife's given name is no concern of yours.

(She shrugs, begins putting the vacuum cleaner back together.)

Louise. Her name was Louise.

CLAUDIA: I'm sorry.

MR. ST. CLARE: How long do you intend to remain here? This is ludicrous.

CLAUDIA: However long it takes, I guess.

MR. ST. CLARE: To what are you alluding?

CLAUDIA: There's one! *(She writes LUDE on the chart.)*

MR. ST. CLARE: Really, Miss Malcolm. The word "allude" is neither lost nor a positive.

CLAUDIA: *De*lude. You know, like to fool yourself? To talk to people who aren't there?

(He gives her a small salute. She beams, puts the marker down, takes the vacuum cleaner and the overflowing bag offstage. He goes to the chart and writes TUIT on the list, returns to the loveseat. She enters, sits beside him. He moves as far away from her as possible, which on the small piece of furniture isn't very far.)

What's *your* first name?

MR. ST. CLARE: You will address me as MR. St. Clare.

CLAUDIA: Peter, right? We used to make jokes about it.

MR. ST. CLARE: I fail to see the humor.

CLAUDIA: It just always seemed so weird to think of you having *any* first name. Peter. Pete.

(She studies him, shakes her head.)

You're right on this one. It's going to have to be MR. St. Clare. Well, MR. St. Clare, the truth is I don't have any place else to go.

(He rises and makes his way to the chart, where he carefully inscribes SOLUTE on the list.)

MR. ST. CLARE: I am sorry to hear that, Miss Malcolm, but of course you cannot stay here.

CLAUDIA: Cannot or may not?

(He writes PUDENT on the list.)

MR. ST. CLARE: Both, in point of fact. This is my home. You simply are not welcome here.

CLAUDIA: We need each other.

MR. ST. CLARE: Hardly.

CLAUDIA: You need me to keep yourself out of a nursing home. I mean, *look* at this place. Your refrigerator is disgusting, and all I found in your cupboards is a few cans of soup and some stale crackers.

MR. ST. CLARE: You have been inspecting my refrigerator and cupboards?

CLAUDIA: And freezer. I found some stuff Louise must've put in there. We'll have chicken cacciatore for dinner.

(He stares at her, then turns and writes SOLENT on the list. She snatches the marker out of his hand and scrawls ERT.)

CLAUDIA: And I need you.

MR. ST. CLARE: What can I do for you?

CLAUDIA: Tell me I haven't wasted my life.

MR. ST. CLARE: Dear God, is that what this is all about?

CLAUDIA: I think they call it unfinished business.

MR. ST. CLARE: And how could I possibly know whether you have wasted your life?

CLAUDIA: Well, shit, MR. St. Clare. If you don't know, who does?

MR. ST. CLARE: Let me get this straight. I am a hostage in my own house. The ransom you have set is an assurance that your life has been worth living. Is that substantially correct?

CLAUDIA: You got it. Substantially.

MR. ST. CLARE: And do I understand correctly that you have a terminal illness of some kind?

(He begins agitatedly moving around the room, picking up his dirty clothes and tossing them into a pile on the floor.)

Miss Malcolm, you are to cease and desist this instant. I did not instruct you—

CLAUDIA: Cancer. A rare kind. My one claim to fame. Too far gone for chemo. I already had surgery—

MR. ST. CLARE: Please, please, spare me the sordid details. All of that is quite irrelevant to the present discussion. Are you in pain? Are there vile excretions of any sort? Are you likely to collapse on my floor?

CLAUDIA: I have blood in my pee.

MR. ST. CLARE: *Miss* Malcolm.

CLAUDIA: The doctor gave me pain pills. A lifetime supply. It's a small bottle.

MR. ST. CLARE: And how long do we have to determine the answer to your question?

CLAUDIA: What do you mean?

MR. ST. CLARE: What is our deadline? *(When she still obviously doesn't understand, he thumps his cane on the floor and assumes the tone he would use with a particularly dense student.)*

How long, Miss Malcolm, will you live?

(She stares at him, then gets down on hands and knees to fish a dirty sock from under the furniture. She holds it up between thumb and forefinger, flings it onto the pile, crosses to the loveseat and searches behind and under it and under its cushions.)

CLAUDIA: Three to six weeks.

MR. ST. CLARE: Not long then. But perhaps long enough. Time pressure can often be an incentive to good work.

(She finds a towel. Clutching it in both hands, she whirls to face him and speaks fiercely.)

CLAUDIA: Listen, dammit. Are you listening? Do I have your attention?

MR. ST. CLARE: I am listening. Miss Claudia Malcolm, you have my complete attention. Speak! *(He waves the cane.)*

CLAUDIA: I'm alone. Never married, no kids, no family. Never done anything that matters. Only ever had crap jobs, nothing that makes any difference to anybody, including me. Don't own a house. Don't have a yard. Shit, I don't even have pets. So what's been the point? *(She buries her face in the towel, discovers it smells bad.)*

MR. ST. CLARE: No one can be sure of the value of his own life, much less someone else's.

(She tosses the towel onto the pile of dirty laundry and sits beside him, forcing him to move to give her room.)

CLAUDIA: *You're* sure, aren't you? About *your* life? How could *you* not be sure? Look at all the lives you've touched with your teaching. Look at all the positives you've rescued.

MR. ST. CLARE: I choose *not* to look at such things, thank you. I would be inundated by angst.

CLAUDIA: INUNDATE!

(They look at each other and both begin to smile. She puts her hand on his arm, and, although he doesn't respond, he also doesn't pull away.)

That's a double, isn't it?

(He moves toward the dictionaries.)

MR. ST. CLARE: We must look it up.

CLAUDIA: No!

MR. ST. CLARE: I beg your pardon?

(She scribbles DATE on the chart.)

CLAUDIA: Screw looking it up! Too late! It's already on the list!

(He pokes at her with the cane.)

MR. ST. CLARE: You forget yourself, Miss Malcolm! I make the rules here!

(She wrests the cane out of his hand and tosses it across the room. He sways and she catches him, holds him by the shoulders and brings her face very close to his.)

CLAUDIA: Tell me I haven't wasted my life. *(Pause. She drops her hands and turns away. He takes a step toward her, stumbles. She catches his hand and he is forced to hold on for support. They continue to hold hands, at arm's length, while he coldly looks her up and down.)*

MR. ST. CLARE: But, Miss Malcolm, that is precisely what you appear to have done.

(Lights down.)

SCENE THREE

Midnight of the same night. The pile of laundry is gone and the dirty dishes have been cleared away. To the chart have been added SCRUTABLE in CLAUDIA's scrawl and SENSICAL in MR. ST. CLARE's script. CLAUDIA is staring at a painting on the wall. MR. ST. CLARE enters, wearing pajamas, an old but still elegant silk dressing gown, and slippers, and leaning more heavily than before on his cane. When he sees her, he straightens. She doesn't turn.

CLAUDIA: Can't sleep either, huh?

MR. ST. CLARE: I am finding it somewhat difficult to relax, yes, under the present circumstances.

(She steps away from the painting, yawning and rubbing her eyes, then suddenly gasps and presses a hand to her lower abdomen.)

Miss Malcolm?

(She waves him off. After a long moment, she straightens, takes a deep breath, eases into a chair.)

CLAUDIA: It's Ms. Well, it's not like you don't have sleep problems when I'm not here. I saw the Sleepytime Tea in your cupboard.

MR. ST. CLARE: As if.

CLAUDIA: It's not *as if* it's my fault. I also found melatonin in your medicine cabinet.

MR. ST. CLARE: My wife was a lifelong insomniac.

(She looks up. Their eyes meet. Then they both move toward the chart. She gets there first and writes SOMNIAC. He makes his way to a chair and settles into it.)

CLAUDIA: So did you love her?

MR. ST. CLARE: Excuse me?

CLAUDIA: Was Louise, you know, your soulmate? The love of your life?

MR. ST. CLARE: We were, for the most part, compatible.

CLAUDIA: When did she die?

MR. ST. CLARE: It has been slightly more than seven months.

CLAUDIA: And you miss her terribly, right?

MR. ST. CLARE: I do not wish to discuss—

(She scrawls CUSS on the list.)

CLAUDIA: Bullshit. It's the middle of the night. Neither one of us has talked to anybody about anything for a long time. Neither one of us is going to live much longer. Give it up, MR. St. Clare. Do you miss her? Is your life empty without her?

MR. ST. CLARE: In truth, my life is not much different without her than it was with her.

CLAUDIA *(pause)*: Well, ain't *that* romantic.

MR. ST. CLARE: Really, Miss Malcolm, I must insist that you refrain from using coarse language in this house.

CLAUDIA: Sorry. AIN'T ain't in the dictionary, right?

MR. ST. CLARE: Actually, I understand that it is in some dictionaries, but only because standards have fallen so abysmally low.

CLAUDIA: Anyway, I know what you mean. About not really loving her.

MR. ST. CLARE: I did not say—

CLAUDIA: Hey, I'm the same way. I've been in love prob-
ably dozens of times, and it's fun and everything, but I don't
think I've ever really loved anybody either. Except you. Isn't
that inane? Oh! *(She writes ANE on the chart.)*

MR. ST. CLARE: Very good, Miss Malcolm, very good
indeed. You have a knack for this. But, of course, schoolgirl
crushes on a male teacher—especially handsome, virile, charis-
matic male teachers—are not unusual.

CLAUDIA: It's not like that. You said something to me that
I never forgot.

MR. ST. CLARE: Saints preserve us. This sort of confession
about how I changed someone's life always arouses in me the
desire to run and hide. Or to purge.

CLAUDIA: I didn't say you changed my life. If you'd
changed my life, would I be here now?

MR. ST. CLARE: I trust that question is rhetorical.

CLAUDIA: Prick.

*(He narrows his eyes. A duel ensues. They read the words aloud
as they write them if the audience can't see the chart well enough. He
inscribes TRAUGHT on the chart. He passes the marker to her, a chal-
lenge. She glares at him for a moment, then scrawls TEST. There fol-
lows a duel: He writes MEMBER; she writes EASE and DIGNANT,
and he shakes his head but lets the words remain and writes TAKE.
She puzzles over that one for a moment, then gets it.)*

CLAUDIA: This is no mistake.

*(She writes APPOINTED. He writes IGNANT. She writes
TREPID. He writes FEATED, and, for the moment, she surrenders.
She tosses the marker onto the desk. Triumphant, he replaces its lid.)*

What I *said* was, you said something to me that I never for-
got. Aren't you curious what it was?

MR. ST. CLARE: Not in the least. Chances are I would not
remember having said it, or I did not, in fact, say it. Former
students seem to have a tendency to create mythologies which
have little or nothing to do with me.

(She stalks to the door, fumbles with the locks.)

CLAUDIA: I'm outta here.

MR. ST. CLARE: Where are you going?

CLAUDIA: What do you care? I don't know. I got better things to do with my three-to-six weeks than play stupid games with you.

MR. ST. CLARE: Such as?

CLAUDIA: Such as walk out in front of a bus.

MR. ST. CLARE: Perhaps it would be wise for you to wait until morning.

CLAUDIA: Why? Because it's not safe? Something might happen to me?

MR. ST. CLARE: It is not seemly for a woman to be out and about at night unescorted.

CLAUDIA: Seemly. Now *there's* a bizarre word.

MR. ST. CLARE: After intruding upon my privacy in such an outrageous manner, you may cook my breakfast. I have had nothing more substantial than cold cereal in nearly seven months.

(She comes back to write TRUDE and RAGEOUS on the chart.)
RAGEOUS?

CLAUDIA: You ever hear of something being *INRAGEOUS*?

MR. ST. CLARE: A bit of a stretch, but I'll accept it.

CLAUDIA: Gee, thanks.

MR. ST. CLARE: I shall give you the money to buy breakfast ingredients. Pancakes and sausage, I think. Juice, coffee. Toast.

(She returns to the door and starts unlocking the locks.)

CLAUDIA: I don't do breakfast. You're on your own with this one.

MR. ST. CLARE: Since we are both unlikely to sleep any more this night, perhaps we should use the time to investigate your query as to the meaning and purpose of your life.

CLAUDIA: You want me to stay?

MR. ST. CLARE: I said no such thing. What I *said* was—

CLAUDIA: What you *said* was: "Even for someone like you, Miss Malcolm, a positive once lost need not remain so." I never forgot that.

MR. ST. CLARE: Perhaps I was a trifle harsh. For effect. To get your attention.

CLAUDIA: "Even you, Miss Malcolm, are probably capable

of participating in this reclaiming exercise, if you put your mind to it."

MR. ST. CLARE: And this made you "love" me?

CLAUDIA: "When you are ready, Miss Malcolm, we shall try it together."

MR. ST. CLARE: And you never did come back to class, did you? You never did accept the challenge.

CLAUDIA: I'm ready now. And there's not much time.

(She sits and folds her hands in her lap. After a moment he goes to stand beside the desk again. He lifts a dictionary off the stack and with great effort tosses it to her. She tries to catch it but misses, and it crashes to the floor. He claps his hand sharply.)

MR. ST. CLARE: Heads up! Pay attention, Miss Malcolm. There is no place in the Society for Lost Positives for students who will not extend themselves.

(Lights down.)

SCENE FOUR

Dawn. CLAUDIA and MR. ST. CLARE are sitting on the loveseat breakfasting on toast and coffee. The chart is full of lost positives such as DOMITABLE, DULATE, CONSOLATE, MUNE, TRANSIGENT, TILL, for the most part alternating between his writing and hers. CLAUDIA speaks with her mouth full.

CLAUDIA: How about ERY!

MR. ST. CLARE: Pardon?

CLAUDIA: ERY. From MISERY.

(Sloshing her coffee as she gulps it, she leaps to her feet and writes the lost positive on the chart. He rises, quickly but with more decorum, and firmly crosses it out.)

CLAUDIA: Why not?

MR. ST. CLARE: The "mis" in the word "misery" has a different etymology. It is not a negative.

CLAUDIA: Could've fooled me.

MR. ST. CLARE: Indeed. Some words which to the linguistically naive might appear to be lost positives are, in fact, not.

(Another duel: She writes, and he immediately crosses out: CIDE, PULSE, ACERBATE, ANIMOUS. Finally they stop, he out of breath and she scowling. He writes IN BREATH on the chart and glares at her as if daring her to dispute him.)

CLAUDIA: God*damn* it, it's not fair! I don't even *like* my life, and I'm *still* scared to death. So to speak. *I'm so scared. (She begins to cry quietly.)*

MR. ST. CLARE: Now, now, none of that.

CLAUDIA: You never did have any patience. You'd reduce somebody to tears and then make fun of them for crying.

MR. ST. CLARE: Did I ever do that to you?

CLAUDIA: All the time. I was a lousy student, and back in those days I cried over every little thing. So I was an easy target.

(He shakes his head and looks down, ashamed. Still with her back turned to him, she doesn't see this. On the bookshelf she notices something and picks it up. We see that it's a poster of sorts, words written in large and elaborate calligraphy on fancy paper, matted and framed like a print.)

What's this?

MR. ST. CLARE: Many years ago, on my fiftieth birthday, someone—a student, I presume, although I never was able to confirm that—left this for me on my desk.

CLAUDIA: And you've kept it all these years.

MR. ST. CLARE: There seemed no point in discarding it. *(He points at her.)*

Did you catch it, Miss Malcolm?

CLAUDIA: Catch what?

MR. ST. CLARE: The lost positive, of course. This *is* the Society for Lost Positives, is it not? CARD? From DISCARD?

(They exchange a smile but neither bothers to write it on the chart. She holds up the poster and reads aloud.)

CLAUDIA: "Find GRUNTLEMENT. Pass it on."

MR. ST. CLARE: Ah, yes, there was a definite shortage of GRUNTLEMENT in my life at the time.

CLAUDIA: I think GRUNTLEMENT's just sort of generally in short supply.

MR. ST. CLARE: I kept this in my desk drawer until I retired.

CLAUDIA: You didn't put it up?

MR. ST. CLARE: Certainly not. It was a private communication.

CLAUDIA: From who?

MR. ST. CLARE: Whom.

CLAUDIA: Whatever.

MR. ST. CLARE: I have never been able to determine the source of the gift. Or how he or she or they knew it was my birthday, and my fiftieth birthday at that, since I certainly never divulged such personal information to my students.

CLAUDIA: Mrs. K. in the office knew all kinds of stuff like that and she'd tell anybody anything if you just chatted with her nice.

MR. ST. CLARE: I suspect one or another of my more gifted students may have misinterpreted my interest as personal. But they have all denied any knowledge of the prank, at the time and in succeeding years when I have questioned them at class reunions and on their pilgrimages to visit me.

CLAUDIA: You didn't just keep it. You kept it where you could look at it.

MR. ST. CLARE: Yes. Well. That anonymous gift meant a good deal to me, if you must know. The fact that someone went to the effort and expense of having it printed, matted, and framed.

CLAUDIA: So what were they trying to tell you?

MR. ST. CLARE: Really, I believe it's rather obvious—

CLAUDIA: Well, *excuse* me all to hell—

MR. ST. CLARE: —that it is an allusion to my having presented myself as perhaps a trifle—stern. I did, in fact, somewhat alter my approach as a result.

CLAUDIA: You did?

MR. ST. CLARE: Somewhat.

CLAUDIA: I heard you mellowed out. No more dictionaries in the face. No more paddling for not having the right answer. I heard you even apologized once for hurting somebody's feelings—

MR. ST. CLARE: You must not believe everything you hear.

CLAUDIA: It was from me.

MR. ST. CLARE: Pardon?

CLAUDIA: The poster was from me.

MR. ST. CLARE: You? I hardly knew you.

CLAUDIA: I knew you, though. At least enough to think you might like it. *(She turns slowly to face him, clutching the poster.)* You did like it, didn't you?

MR. ST. CLARE: I—yes…Thank you, Miss Malcolm.

CLAUDIA: You're welcome. *(She puts the poster back in its place.)*

You know, we *are* sort of getting personal here. You *could* call me "Claudia."

MR. ST. CLARE: "Miss Malcolm" will do nicely.

CLAUDIA: It's Ms. You are incorrigible, you know that?

(He looks up sharply, smiles, and starts to get up. She stops him.) Don't bother. What's the point?

(He hesitates, then scowls and proceeds. She watches with annoyance while he painstakingly adds CORRIGIBLE and then PLICIT, and TRACT. Triumphantly, he replaces the marker and turns to glare at her. She has reached her limit.)

You know what? This is not where I want to spend any more of my time.

(She starts toward the door again. He moves to block her way, isn't quite fast enough, sticks his cane out in front of her.)

MR. ST. CLARE: Don't go.

CLAUDIA: Why?

MR. ST. CLARE: You have not been excused.

CLAUDIA: Watch me.

(She starts to unlock the door. He thumps his way up close beside her, but makes no move to touch her.)

MR. ST. CLARE: Miss Malcolm. I must insist that you complete the assignment.

CLAUDIA: What are you talking about?

MR. ST. CLARE: The reason you gave for this home invasion was to determine whether your life had had value. I would submit that you have not yet made that determination.

CLAUDIA: Sure I have.

MR. ST. CLARE: You are being too hasty. You are giving up too soon. All worthwhile endeavors require time and effort. Simply because we have not yet discerned—

(He acknowledges the lost positive with a nod.)

—discerned any value to your life, you ought not assume—

CLAUDIA: No, actually, I got what I came for. *(She takes down the GRUNTLEMENT poster.)*

Can I have this? I need it more than you do.

MR. ST. CLARE: Absolutely not. That has sat on my bookshelf for thirty-odd years.

CLAUDIA: I won't need it long. I'll will it back to you.

MR. ST. CLARE *(pause)*: Very well. Yes. You *may* have it.

(She gives him a quick kiss on the cheek.)

CLAUDIA: Good-bye, MR. St. Clare. Thanks for everything.

(She exits. Pause. Then he takes up his position again in front of the desk and the chart. At first his voice breaks and he stumbles a bit, but he gains strength and conviction as he goes along.)

MR. ST. CLARE: This meeting of the Society for Lost Positives will now come to order. We will begin with the payment of dues. Who has come prepared with a lost positive in need of reclaiming? Miss Malcolm? Would you care to begin? What's that? TIMACY? From INTIMACY? The etymology is highly questionable, Miss Malcolm, highly suspect. But for the purposes of discussion—

(He adds TIMACY to the list on the chart.)

—What's that? T-E-R-Y. From MYSTERY? No, no, Miss Malcolm. The "mys" in MYSTERY is clearly not a negative. I'm afraid that will not do. *(Pause.)* Very well, very well. I will accept that. INTIMACY and MYSTERY. *(Pause.)* Thank you, Miss Malcolm.

(Lights down.)

END OF PLAY

TURNING LEFT

A PLAY IN ONE ACT

Production History

Turning Left had a staged reading in 2006 for the Colorado Dramatists, Denver, Colorado.

Characters

JUDITH, professional woman, age late forties, partially blind.
DELIA, Judith's mother, age late seventies, crotchety.
SKI GUIDE, either gender (although a male voice would be a nice contrast), age mid-twenties, cheery and encouraging.

SCENE ONE

At rise, DELIA is sitting in the chair.

(JUDITH enters, gives DELIA a peck on the cheek.)
JUDITH: Hi, how are you today?
DELIA: Fine, thanks, how are you?
JUDITH: Guess what I did yesterday? *(Pause.)* I went skiing!
DELIA: Skiing. Well, for heaven's sake.
JUDITH: It's a program to teach blind people to ski. I finally got up the nerve to try it.
DELIA: You're not blind!
JUDITH: Close enough.
DELIA: You're forty-seven years old. You've got a family and a job, responsibilities. Why would you take up some silly thing like skiing?
JUDITH: No, see, what I want to hear from you is, "That's great, Judith. I admire your spirit, Judith. I'm proud of you for doing something that scares you, Judith."
DELIA: You ought to know better, a woman your age.
(JUDITH shakes her head and exits to the kitchen.)
Skiing. For heaven's sake.
(DELIA busies herself around the room. JUDITH returns with a tray, moving slowly so as not to bump into anything. As she starts to put the tray down on the table, DELIA rushes to move things out of her way, thereby making the path more complicated.)
JUDITH *(lightly)*: Oh, thanks. I wouldn't have seen that.
DELIA: Don't talk about that!
JUDITH: About what?
DELIA: About not seeing things.
JUDITH: That's part of who I am.

DELIA: That's what's so hard to take.

JUDITH: Look. You took that medication because at the time they thought it prevented miscarriages. How could I blame you for that?

DELIA: It's not that.

JUDITH: What then? You mean when you fell down the basement steps while you were pregnant with me? My ophthalmologist says that didn't cause it.

(DELIA says nothing. JUDITH pours juice. DELIA accepts it but doesn't drink.)

Oh, come on. Prune juice isn't that bad. The doctor said it might help.

(DELIA sips, makes a face. JUDITH doesn't see her holding the glass out.)

DELIA: Take it! I don't want it!

JUDITH: Will you eat a bran muffin? I baked them especially for you.

DELIA: I don't want it.

JUDITH: Suit yourself. I've got to get to work.

DELIA: I can't see that your bran muffins and prune juice are making a bit of difference.

JUDITH: I don't know what else to do. I hope the doctor calls with the test results before I have to leave.

DELIA: It hurts.

JUDITH: I know. I'm sorry. *(JUDITH consumes the muffin and juice herself, makes a face.)*

Have you ever noticed that I don't have a name for you?

DELIA: Well, for heaven's sake.

JUDITH: I say "my mother" when I'm talking about you, but I don't address you as "Mom" or "Mother" or anything. Don't you think that's odd?

DELIA: When you were little you called me "Mommy."

JUDITH: Are you sure? I don't remember that. I do remember how you used to tell me the reason people stared at me was because I was so pretty. I knew it was a lie, but it was such a loving lie it made me feel good anyway. *(Pause.)* Thank you.

DELIA: I don't remember that.

JUDITH: One of the most important things you ever did for

me, it affected my whole life, and you don't remember it?

DELIA: That was a long time ago.

JUDITH: How did you and Daddy know how to raise a handicapped child? You didn't have any role models, did you? Or anybody to ask for advice? I was always the only disabled kid in school.

DELIA: Don't say that word!

JUDITH: What word? Handicapped? Disabled? I'm not ashamed of it. Why are you?

DELIA: I just don't want to talk about it!

JUDITH: Well, I do.

(The phone rings. DELIA doesn't move.)

It's probably the doctor.

DELIA: It's too early in the morning to talk on the phone.

JUDITH: I'll get it.

(Hurrying, JUDITH bumps into the door frame as she exits. DELIA covers her face with her hands for a moment, then gets up and begins making the bed, dusting, etc. JUDITH returns.)

That was the doctor.

DELIA: Would you look at those cobwebs? Get me that long-handled feather duster.

(JUDITH hesitates, then exits. DELIA continues straightening the room until JUDITH returns without the duster.)

JUDITH: I can't find it.

DELIA: Well, for heaven's sake! If it was a snake it would've bit you!

(As DELIA starts to exit, JUDITH catches her by the shoulders. DELIA flinches.)

JUDITH: Let's sit down.

DELIA: Some of us don't have time to sit. The house is filthy and the leaves need raked—

JUDITH: It's cancer.

DELIA: No, it's not. The doctor said it wasn't anything to worry about.

JUDITH: She's shocked. But the tests show it's cancer.

DELIA: Standing here gabbing with you is not going to get this house cleaned. And don't you have to get on to work?

(DELIA exits. JUDITH covers her face with her hands in a gesture

echoing her mother's, then puts on her coat and exits. Lights down.)

SCENE TWO

Next morning. At rise, DELIA stands with her hands on her belly and an expression of pain on her face. When JUDITH enters with gro-ceries, DELIA hastily busies herself.

JUDITH: Good morning.

DELIA: Well, good morning. I was worried.

JUDITH: Why?

DELIA: Why, it's almost noon.

JUDITH: Oh, the kids had dental appointments, and the buses don't run as often on Saturdays. Then I stopped by the store and picked up apples and bread.

DELIA: Never did like apples.

JUDITH: Really? Why didn't I know that?

DELIA: There are lots of things you don't know about me.

JUDITH *(sharply)*: And that's just the way you like it.

DELIA: We...for heaven's sake. Talking to your mother like that.

(JUDITH exits to put the groceries in the kitchen. DELIA begins furiously cleaning out the closet. JUDITH returns, stumbles over a pile of things DELIA has pulled out.)

Oh, oh, be careful!

JUDITH: No big deal. Don't panic.

DELIA *(panicking)*: Are you all right?

JUDITH: I just stumbled. Now that I'm a skier, I'll be doing a lot worse than that.

DELIA: Aren't you frightened?

JUDITH: Yes. I've never done this before. *(JUDITH would say more but DELIA waves her off and resumes cleaning out the closet.)* Can I help?

DELIA: Go through those boxes and see what you want. *(Beat.)* How long?

JUDITH: How long what?

DELIA: You know. What the doctor said.

JUDITH: She said—maybe two months.

DELIA: Months.

JUDITH: It's not operable. She said chemo might buy you a little time, but it would be awfully hard on you.

DELIA: I'm not doing that.

JUDITH: Well, maybe you should think about it—

(*DELIA tosses out more things.*)

DELIA: Here's more junk.

JUDITH: Look at all this. I never thought of you as sentimental.

DELIA: Trash bags are under the sink.

JUDITH: What did you do, keep every report card and school paper?

DELIA: You know, they told us to send you away to a special boarding school because regular school would be too hard for you.

JUDITH: It wasn't.

DELIA: You always were smart. Just like your father. He said your mind saved you.

JUDITH: I'm glad you stood up to the experts.

DELIA: Your father thought you'd be better off at home.

JUDITH: And what did you think?

DELIA: I was afraid the other children would make fun of you.

JUDITH: Nobody ever did. It's really sort of amazing. Even though I had to hold things so close to read it probably looked like I was smelling them.

DELIA: I hated that you were different.

JUDITH: It was okay.

DELIA: There's a box of hats in the back of the closet. Take them for the girls for dress-up.

JUDITH: They're twelve and fifteen. I don't think so.

DELIA: Fine.

(*DELIA goes back into the closet and starts tossing things out. JUDITH removes papers from a box.*)

JUDITH: You and Daddy made me believe I was fine just the way I was. Didn't you mean that?

(*DELIA doesn't respond.*)

Were you ashamed of me?

(DELIA doesn't respond.)

I'll take the hats.

(DELIA doesn't respond. JUDITH removes a manila envelope from the box and pulls a newspaper clipping out of the envelope.)

What's this envelope full of newspaper clippings?

(DELIA rushes to retrieve them.)

DELIA: That's not yours—

JUDITH *(reading)*: "Miss Delia Montgomery and Mr. Lloyd Bradley were joined in holy matrimony on March 3, 1939." You were married to somebody else before Daddy?

DELIA: Yes.

JUDITH: Why did I never know this? Did Daddy know?

DELIA: He said he'd marry me anyway, but we couldn't tell anybody. When you were born he made me promise not to tell you. Especially not you.

JUDITH: But you kept the article. "The bride wore a white silk suit and a corsage of yellow orchids."

DELIA: I meant to throw all that out.

JUDITH: So tell me about this Lloyd Bradley guy.

DELIA: This box goes out in the trash.

(JUDITH sighs and exits with the box. DELIA is dusting around the window sill when suddenly she cries out and drops the duster to clutch one hand with the other. JUDITH enters and hurries to her, bumping into things that are out of place.)

JUDITH: What's wrong? Are you in pain?

DELIA: I got stung! By a bee! Look!

(JUDITH takes DELIA's hand and raises it close to her eyes.)

JUDITH: I don't see anything.

(DELIA tries to snatch her hand away but JUDITH won't let her.)

It does feel a little hot and swollen. I don't see the stinger, but I bet there's bee poison in there.

DELIA: I've never been stung by a bee before.

JUDITH: In your whole life? You've been lucky. Remember the time I knocked over a wasp nest and a swarm of them chased me?

DELIA: I don't remember that.

JUDITH: I was screaming and pounding on the door and then you came and rescued me.

DELIA: I didn't keep you from getting into the nest in the first place, though, did I? Didn't make sure the door was unlocked.

JUDITH: You calmed me down. You comforted me. You said, "The worst is over now. You've made it through the worst."

DELIA: I'm seventy-six years old and I get stung by a bee for the first time in my life. It's not fair.

JUDITH: I don't know if "fair" has anything to do with it.

DELIA: It hurts!

JUDITH: I know. I'm sorry.

DELIA: And now I have—

(DELIA can't say the word. JUDITH tries to hug her but DELIA pulls away and exits.

Lights down.)

SCENE THREE

JUDITH on skis, wearing goggles and a bright orange vest that reads "Blind Skier." Clutching poles, she inches her way down a gentle slope.

GUIDE *(voice only)*: Lookin' great, Judith!

(JUDITH falls, struggles to her feet, tries again.)

That's it! Don't look at your skis!

JUDITH: My tips keep crossing! I'm afraid I'll fall!

GUIDE: You will fall. If you never fall, you aren't doing it right.

JUDITH: Too fast! Too fast!

GUIDE: Stay with it! Hey, Judith, don't look now but you're skiing!

JUDITH: I'm skiing!

(JUDITH continues down the slope.)

I made it!

(JUDITH raises her poles in triumph and falls, laughing. Lights down.)

SCENE FOUR

Two days later. Unmade bed, a flower arrangement on the table.

JUDITH and DELIA enter. DELIA has been raking leaves.

JUDITH *(entering):* —why don't you hire somebody to rake the leaves.

DELIA: Pay good money when I'm still perfectly capable—

JUDITH: Or let me do it.

DELIA: You might hurt yourself.

JUDITH: With a leaf rake? I'm perfectly capable—

DELIA: I don't want to talk about this.

JUDITH: It's because of you and Daddy that I can do things, you know. It's because of you that I'm skiing.

(DELIA collects clothes from the closet and exits with them. JUDITH spreads the contents of the manila envelope and regards them, then notices the flowers.)

Where'd the flowers come from?

(DELIA enters.)

They're pretty. Do you have a secret admirer?

DELIA: Well, for heaven's sake.

JUDITH: So who sent you flowers?

DELIA: My sister.

JUDITH: Aunt Maureen? How nice.

DELIA: She only sent them because she thinks I'm sick.

JUDITH: She sent them because she loves you.

DELIA: I don't want them. Throw them out.

(DELIA furiously begins stripping the bed. Reaching to retrieve the papers, JUDITH bumps into her. Both mutter apologies. JUDITH lays the papers down and helps DELIA. As the scene continues, they work together to make the bed.)

JUDITH: Tell me about Lloyd Bradley. *(Pause.)* Your first husband.

DELIA: You always were so stubborn!

JUDITH: Was he—abusive?

DELIA: He ran around.

JUDITH: Oh.

DELIA: I had quite a few suitors, and he was the one Dad didn't like.

JUDITH: You married a man your parents didn't like. Some things never change.

DELIA: I like Mark.

JUDITH: You and Daddy didn't want me to marry him. You thought he couldn't "support" me because he's an artist.

DELIA: Well, in case you couldn't work.

JUDITH: But of course I can "support" myself. And Mark's a good man. Was Lloyd Bradley a good man?

(Long pause. Then DELIA explodes.)

DELIA: I've always had the devil in me! Always! Lloyd Bradley knew it! My father knew it! Every time I look at you I see it, ever since you were born! And now, now, I have—

(JUDITH starts toward her, stops when DELIA waves her off. DELIA buries her face in a pillow and sobs. Lights down.)

SCENE FIVE

SEVERAL WEEKS LATER.

At rise, DELIA is in the rocking chair staring out the window. JUDITH enters with a tray.

JUDITH: Do you think you could eat some pudding?

DELIA: I don't know.

(JUDITH sets the tray too close to the edge and nearly spills everything.)

Be careful!

JUDITH: Did I ever tell you about my first date with Mark? I took him to dinner at a fancy restaurant, white linen tablecloths, tall crystal wine glasses, white wine. I was going to impress this guy, right? So I poured. Right down the side of the glass in a puddle on the table. He was so amazed he just sat there and watched me do it. And he married me anyway. *(JUDITH laughs. DELIA does not.)*

DELIA: In my day, a woman didn't take a man to dinner.

JUDITH (Pause): Here. Tell me how this pudding tastes. You have to eat something.

(DELIA grudgingly accepts the dish but doesn't eat. After a moment JUDITH begins to feed her.)

Are you having pain today?

DELIA: Not so much pain as pressure.

JUDITH: You actually had more pain with the bee sting, didn't you?

DELIA: Maybe the doctor's wrong.

JUDITH: She asked if I wanted her to tell you. I thought I should be the one. *(Pause.)* It was a really hard thing to say to you.

DELIA: Are you going skiing this weekend?

JUDITH: Sunday. Mark and the kids will come over.

DELIA: I just want to put you in a cage so nothing will happen to you.

JUDITH: Believe me, at the speed I go, if I ran into a tree neither one of us would be the worse. *(Pause.)* You know, you're not alone in this.

DELIA: I've always been alone.

JUDITH: You had Daddy. And me. And three grandchildren. By the way, I talked to Aunt Maureen last night.

DELIA: Why?

JUDITH: She called to see how you were. She thought you'd be offended if she called you, like you were about the flowers. I asked her about Lloyd Bradley. She said he used to frequent whore houses and Grandpa'd have to bring him home. Hard to imagine the elegant old man doing that.

DELIA: Whenever I look at you I see my shame. I see that devil that's in me.

JUDITH: Great. *(Pause.)* Does this have something to do with Lloyd Bradley?

DELIA: I don't want to talk about it!

(DELIA pushes herself up, gets dizzy. JUDITH catches her.)

The kitchen floor needs mopping—

JUDITH: Are you scared?

DELIA: Scared?

JUDITH: Of—of what's happening to you?

(DELIA exits.)
I mean, neither one of us has ever done this before.
(Lights down.)

SCENE SIX

At rise, JUDITH is on the slope, trying to learn how to turn.

GUIDE *(voice only)*: Try it again. Turn your head to the right and your body will follow.
(JUDITH executes a clumsy right turn.)
There it is! Your first right turn!
JUDITH: Yes!!
GUIDE: Now a left turn.
JUDITH: Oh, I don't—
GUIDE: Weight on your left foot.
(JUDITH tries to follow the directions.)
Bring the right ski forward. Look left. There you go!
(JUDITH's head swivels away from the left, bringing her abruptly out of the turn.)
JUDITH: I can't! I can't see on the left side, so in real life I don't turn left if I can avoid it.
GUIDE: This is real life.
JUDITH: This is skiing.
GUIDE: Exactly.
JUDITH: Turning left means using my blindness to turn into the unknown.
GUIDE: Are you ready to try it again?
(As JUDITH begins to make a left turn, her head turns right as if of its own volition and she begins to lose her balance.)
Look left. Follow my voice. Let yourself turn toward my voice.
(JUDITH falls.)
JUDITH: I can't do this. It's too hard. It's too scary.
GUIDE: Do you want to stop?
JUDITH: I want to ski. I just don't want to turn left.
GUIDE: If you're going to ski you have to turn left sometime.
JUDITH: I don't see why.

(She gets up, tries again.)

GUIDE: Don't think about it. Just let it happen.

JUDITH: I'm turning!

GUIDE: Just let the mountain take you. That's it. Turn left, Judith, turn left!

(JUDITH turns left. She and the GUIDE yell triumphantly. Lights down.)

SCENE SEVEN

A few weeks later.

At rise, JUDITH is bathing DELIA in bed.

DELIA: You shouldn't have to clean up your mother.

JUDITH: Why not? You did it for me.

DELIA: You were a baby.

JUDITH: I was two months old when you found out about my eyes, right?

DELIA: Your father wouldn't believe it at first. I knew I wouldn't have a normal child.

(JUDITH knocks things over on the bedside table, finds the lotion and applies some to her own hands, then takes her mother's to rub some onto them.)

JUDITH *(carefully)*: My ophthalmologist says the most likely cause of a visual condition like mine is a virus in the mother. Did you have measles while you were carrying me?

DELIA: No. *(DELIA cries out.)* It burns!

(JUDITH fumbles for pain medication. DELIA cries out again. JUDITH finds the medication, gives it to DELIA with a dropper. DELIA calms. JUDITH resumes bathing her.)

JUDITH: You're crying. Is the pain—I'll give you more—

DELIA: I know why this is happening to me.

JUDITH: It happens to everybody, one way or another.

DELIA: He brought home filth to me.

JUDITH: Who did?

DELIA: He brought home disease, and it's been in me ever since.

JUDITH *(beginning to understand)*: Lloyd Bradley caught a venereal disease from the prostitutes and he infected you.

DELIA: I'm sorry, Judith! All your life I've wanted to tell you that. I'm so sorry.

JUDITH: It's okay. It's always been okay.

DELIA: I deserved it, but not you. Not my perfect little girl.

JUDITH: Why did you deserve it? All you did was marry the wrong guy.

DELIA: My father knew it. He always knew I was dirty. That's why he— *(Pause.)*

(JUDITH realizes what DELIA is trying to tell her.)

JUDITH: Oh, God. Aunt Maureen said you were Grandpa's favorite.

DELIA: I was born with the devil in me, and Dad knew it.

JUDITH: No. Listen to me.

(JUDITH lies down on the bed and takes DELIA in her arms. At first DELIA resists, then relaxes. They are both crying. Lights down.)

SCENE EIGHT

The next day.

At rise, DELIA is in bed, in and out of consciousness. JUDITH paces, now and then pausing to tend to her mother.

JUDITH: Now's the time I ought to say something meaningful. But I never have known what to say to you. I've never even known what to call you.

DELIA: Well, for heaven's sake.

JUDITH: I thought you were—asleep.

DELIA: Show me.

JUDITH: Show you what?

DELIA: Ski.

JUDITH: Show you how I ski?

DELIA: Come here. Show me. Ski.

(Bumping into things, JUDITH makes her way to DELIA's bedside. She acts out what she describes.)

JUDITH: Well, this is how you stand on skis when you're

a rank beginner. It feels weird and looks ridiculous. A lot of skiing is counter-intuitive. For instance, if you lean back when you're going downhill, instead of steadying yourself you'll fall backward. The idea is to go with the mountain. "Trust the mountain," they keep telling me. The hardest thing for me is turning left, because I've never had vision on the left side.

DELIA: Don't—don't talk about that!

JUDITH: You wanted me to show you how I ski. This is how I ski. Turning left is turning into the unknown, every time. I have to get out of the way and let it happen. Trust the mountain.

(JUDITH turns left. Pause. JUDITH resumes pacing.)

Talk about rank beginners. I'm doing the best I can here.

(JUDITH sits on the bed, smooths her mother's brow, adjusts the covers. She lays her hand on DELIA's chest, bends close to feel for breathing. DELIA puts her arms around JUDITH's neck.)

Turn left. Oh, Mama. Mama, turn left.

END OF PLAY

COUSINS

A SHORT PLAY

Characters

OLIVIA, middle-aged, walks with a pronounced limp
JANE, Olivia's cousin, four months younger, no limp

Time and Place

Jane's living room, present.

At rise, Olivia is looking at family photos on the walls, singing under her breath and moving to the rhythm of 60s music playing in the background. Her limp is obvious, and her gait is audibly uneven; now and then she thumps while executing an approximation of a dance step. The music continues throughout the play.

(JANE enters with a tray. OLIVIA indicates a picture on the wall.)

OLIVIA: I have this photo of the two of us with Grandpa, too. We're—what? Maybe thirteen?

JANE: Fourteen. It's dated on the back. Coffee?

OLIVIA: Thanks. So he died just a year later. Remember the funeral? All that incense and the tall hats?

JANE: We were eighteen. Fall of senior year. Cookie?

OLIVIA: Thanks. We were fifteen. I had to miss a dress rehearsal for the funeral, and I was only in drama sophomore year. Mmm, good cookies. I'd love the recipe.

JANE: It's Grandpa's. He used to make them whenever we came to visit, remember? We thought they were gross.

OLIVIA: We did? Are you sure that wasn't some other cousin?

JANE: We're the only girl cousins we've got, cousin.

OLIVIA: Well, they're not gross now. Will you send me the recipe?

JANE: I'll copy it for you before you leave.

OLIVIA: Now they'll remind me of Grandpa.

JANE: I remember because it was such a hard time for me anyway. You were going off to college when you graduated. I didn't have a clue what to do with my life.

OLIVIA: I think about what it must have been like for Grandpa. A teenager, coming to this country all by himself, not a word of English, never seeing his family again—

JANE: He was twenty-one.

OLIVIA: He was seventeen. I have the obituary where it tells about that.

JANE: So do I. Somewhere.

(They laugh, a little annoyed with each other.)

It's good to see you after all these years.

OLIVIA: You, too. We used to come visit every summer. Never took any other vacation.

JANE: We'd always go to the zoo.

OLIVIA AND JANE: And the Smithsonian.

OLIVIA: I hate zoos. And I'm embarrassed to admit I thought the Smithsonian Institute was bo-o-oring.

JANE: Are you serious? I always looked forward to it. It was the only time we ever went anywhere, when you came to visit.

OLIVIA: I suppose I ought to give the Smithsonian another chance.

JANE: I found this old album.

(They look at photos.)

JANE: Oh, look at us!

OLIVIA: We must be about two.

JANE: Aren't we cute? Those little matching coats and bonnets!

OLIVIA: We don't Look all that happy.

JANE: You don't look all that happy. I'm smiling.

OLIVIA: You did something to me. Off-camera. Pinched me or something.

JANE: I did not!

(They're both trying to pretend they're not getting upset.)

OLIVIA: You were mean to me. You were. Look, see? My face is all scrunched up.

JANE: Sun in your eyes.

OLIVIA: No! You did something mean to me! You were always doing something mean to me! Every time we were together! Look, see? Here's another picture, and I'm crying and you're laughing.

JANE: Guess I was the good-natured cousin.

OLIVIA: You were not good-natured, you were mean!

JANE: Be right back.

(Jane exits. Olivia looks at photos, by turns smiling and looking indignant. Jane enters.)

Can't find the obituary. But I did find this. *(Jane holds up a tattered restaurant menu.)*

Remember the trip to Quebec?

OLIVIA: Oh, God, yes. The bachelor party we just happened into?

JANE: Bachelor party?

OLIVIA: They didn't speak English and you didn't speak French and I spoke just enough to keep saying *"Non,* non, *absolutment* no!"

JANE: I have no memory of—

OLIVIA: Oh, please. You have no memory of taking off in the car with one of those guys and leaving me stranded in the hotel room with the rest of them?

(Their annoyance with each other is growing.)

JANE: I would never—

OLIVIA: Nothing bad happened, no thanks to you. They weren't rapists, just out for a good time. They called me a cab back to the hotel.

JANE: You're making this up.

OLIVIA: I pretended to be asleep when you came in in the middle of the night.

JANE: Didn't happen.

OLIVIA: It did! I was mad about that for years. Maybe I still am a little.

JANE: I'm sorry. Even though I didn't—

OLIVIA: You did!

(They laugh too loudly.)

JANE: What I remember about that trip is all the artists in the streets.

OLIVIA: I don't remember artists.

JANE: I'd never seen anything like that before. Made me want to move to Quebec and be a street artist.

OLIVIA: You never did, did you? I'd have heard—

JANE: Never lived anyplace but here.

OLIVIA: Why didn't you?

JANE: I'm the timid cousin, remember? Plain Jane. You got

all the adventurousness. Published writer and everything.

OLIVIA: I'm sorry. I guess.

JANE: You took notes on that trip.

OLIVIA: Nobody's safe around a writer.

JANE: Made me really self-conscious.

OLIVIA: Well, I did write a story. Called "Cousin Joan."

JANE: Great.

OLIVIA: Probably shouldn't tell you that.

JANE: Yeah, probably not.

OLIVIA: I can send you a copy of the magazine where it was published.

JANE: Uh, no. Thanks.

OLIVIA: We were twenty-two. Right?

JANE: You were. I was twenty-one. It was the summer between our birthdays.

OLIVIA: That's right. I'm four months older.

JANE: Which is how you got my name.

OLIVIA: What name?

JANE: Our mothers talked about names when they were pregnant with us. My mom told your mom I was going to be Olivia.

OLIVIA: For Olivia de Havilland.

JANE: But you were born first and you stole it.

OLIVIA: I didn't—my parents—

JANE: So, I got Jane for Jane Russell. Not even a "y" like Jayne Mansfield.

OLIVIA: Jane's a nice name.

JANE: I was supposed to be Olivia.

OLIVIA *(laughing)*: I'm—sorry. Can you forgive me?

JANE *(not laughing)*: Haven't yet.

OLIVIA *(sobering)*: Really, Jane, I'm sorry. That was a nasty thing for my parents to do.

JANE: Used to think it ruined my life.

(Pause. Olivia resumes looking at photos.)

OLIVIA: Can't believe you have this one.

JANE: We're seven or eight. That's my bedroom in the old house. I was seven when we moved. *(She looks challengingly at Olivia.)*

OLIVIA: See how you're making fun of me?

JANE: I am not! I wouldn't—

OLIVIA: Caught right there on film. No use denying it.

(The tension between them has increased.)

JANE: What are you talking about?

OLIVIA: Look! You're standing behind me copying the way I walk. And grinning.

JANE: I wasn't—

OLIVIA: You're lopsided at exactly the same angle and your left leg is bent so it's shorter than your right one and your right elbow is sticking out just like mine! That's deliberate, Jane! That's mean!

JANE: I wasn't making fun of you!

OLIVIA: Bullshit! What else could that be?

JANE: I wanted to feel what it was like to be you! I wanted to be you! *(Pause.)*

OLIVIA: Really? Why?

JANE: Because you were everything I wanted to be! You were my hero!

(Long pause. Olivia stands, a bit awkwardly, and holds out her hands to Jane.)

OLIVIA: Hey, girl cousin. Wanna dance?

(Jane hesitates, then takes Olivia's hands. They dance, Olivia's gait setting the pace and rhythm.)

Lights down. Sounds of their laughter and Olivia's thumping. Music keeps playing.

END OF PLAY

COMFORT ME WITH PEACHES

A PLAY IN TWO ACTS

Based on the journals of Roberta Robertson

Production History

Comfort Me With Peaches received a full production at the Academy Theatre in Meadville, Pennsylvania, May 7-9, 2010. The play also received staged readings at the Federal Theatre in Denver Colorado in 2006, and at the Victorian Playhouse in Denver Colorado in 2008.

Characters

ALTHEA, an 85-year-old woman
PAM, a 55-year-old woman
HEATHER, a woman in her early thirties
JORDAN, a young teenage girl, PAM's granddaughter
BURT & TRISTAN, offstage characters who do not speak

Time and Place

Present day, ALTHEA's living room in the house where she's lived for more than half a century.

Note
Excerpts from ALTHEA's journals, spoken or read by her or the other characters, are in *italic*.

ACT I

Lights up on ALTHEA's living room: Couch, table and chairs, notebooks and loose papers, a toybox, a doll with elastic on hands and feet so a child could dance with it. Sound of a vacuum cleaner offstage.

ALTHEA enters peeling a banana, crosses stage, exits to BURT's room, leaving the peel on the table. Vacuum cleaner stops. PAM enters, puts banana peel in trash bag, exits. ALTHEA enters, looks for banana peel, then sits at the table and writes in a notebook. HEATHER enters.

HEATHER: Let's check this curl.

(ALTHEA closes the notebook. HEATHER unrolls a curler on top, rolls it back up.)

Your hair does *not* want to take this curl.

(JORDAN enters wearing headphones, dusting with a long-handled feather duster.)

ALTHEA *(to HEATHER)*: I'm surprised you could even find enough to roll.

HEATHER: Remember how you used to come over every Saturday morning and set my Aunt Mabel's hair?

ALTHEA: Mabel was a sweet old lady. Interesting, too. Not long before she died she said to me, "I haven't done much with my life," and I said, "Mabel, you're one of the most successful people I know, because of the kind of person you are." Why do you suppose they call it a "permanent" when you have to get one every few months?

HEATHER: Well, it's more permanent than if you didn't have a permanent.

ALTHEA: Relatively permanent, I guess. Like relatively pregnant or relatively alive.

HEATHER: My brother Jonathan says everything's relative. Like he's not as sick as some people he knows. He is such an idiot.

ALTHEA: How is Jonathan? He was always such a nice little boy.

HEATHER: Oh, he's just fine. Considering he's got AIDS.

ALTHEA: AIDS is such a terrible scourge.

HEATHER: Never been anything like it before.

ALTHEA: You hardly ever hear of scarlet fever or diphtheria or bubonic plague anymore, and they were the dread diseases of their day. I suppose there'll be a cure or a vaccine for AIDS, too, some time or other.

HEATHER: So? My brother's got it *now*.

ALTHEA: I had a burst appendix in 1945, just after penicillin became available outside the military. A year earlier and I'd surely have died. If Jonathan can just hang on—

(PAM enters with the vacuum cleaner.)

PAM: Okay, Althea, I'll just do the bathroom—Jordan? You about through dusting?

(JORDAN doesn't hear her over the music through her headphones. She comes upon some of ALTHEA's diaries and pages through them.)

ALTHEA: I had a banana peel and I don't know what became of it.

PAM: I put it in the trash.

ALTHEA: It goes in the compost. I just left it there while I took Burt his morning banana.

PAM: Jordan. Those are Althea's private papers.

ALTHEA: I was thinking the other day: I've been keeping a diary for sixty-nine years.

PAM: Oral history. I still have that book we did together with my class, how many years ago?

ALTHEA: I remember there was a little blonde-haired girl named Annie. That was my mother's name.

PAM: Twenty-some years later I had her son, and when Annie came in for a parent-teacher conference she brought her copy of our book.

ALTHEA: Is it strange, having the children of the children you taught?

PAM: I'm starting to have their grandchildren!

ALTHEA: Sixty-nine years. It's hard to believe *anything* happened to me sixty-nine years ago. And in some places I was writing about things that had taken place years before that even.

PAM: That was my first year teaching. A long time ago. Not sixty-nine years, but a long time. I've done that project every year since. It started a lot of things.

ALTHEA: Our friendship, for one.

PAM: And my writing. Two of the most important things in my life.

ALTHEA: There've been a lot of changes over those years, but it seems to me at heart people's lives are pretty much the same. Jordan, do you keep a diary?

JORDAN: What? I mean, pardon?

ALTHEA: Do you keep a diary? A lot of girls do. Or used to, anyway.

JORDAN: Online.

ALTHEA: On the internet, you mean? Doesn't that defeat the purpose of a diary—to keep secrets?

JORDAN: You don't give your password to anybody but your friends.

ALTHEA: And the other purpose—to record things for posterity?

JORDAN: For who?

(ALTHEA starts to explain, is interrupted by PAM exiting with the cleaning supplies. JORDAN opens another notebook.)

HEATHER *(exits)*: I need a smoke.

ALTHEA: I wrote something about secrets and diaries when I was just a little older than you. It would have been in about 1936.

ALTHEA and JORDAN: *Today I told mama I thought Georgia had read my whole diary.*

JORDAN: *And I bet she hadn't kept it a secret, either. I don't think mama will say anything to her, so I went and sat up in the peach tree and wrote me a poem.*

ALTHEA:
Comfort me with peaches
For I am sick of love.

I used to be as lovesick
As a turtle dove.
But now I'm tired of kisses.
I'm tired of sisters, too,
Who go and read my diary
To find out what I do.

JORDAN: Omigod, that is so immature!

ALTHEA: *Georgia, I wrote that just for you. I hope you like it. And by the way, anybody who reads my diary is a big sneak!*

JORDAN: Who's Georgia?

ALTHEA: My little sister.

JORDAN: How old is she?

ALTHEA: Eighty-two.

JORDAN: Your *little* sister is eighty-two? That is so weird!

ALTHEA: It is sort of weird, isn't it?

JORDAN: I've got a little sister.

ALTHEA: Your grandma's mentioned her. I'd like to meet her.

JORDAN: She lives in Texas with her dad. I get to see her, like, once a year or something.

ALTHEA: Actually, I have three little sisters. I don't see them very often, either. Which is just as well.

JORDAN: I've always wanted a brother.

ALTHEA: I had three of those, too.

JORDAN: How old are they? Like a hundred?

ALTHEA: They've all died.

JORDAN *(beat)*: Oh.

ALTHEA: It's strange to think of. I remember writing in my diary: Life is queer.

JORDAN: Queer?!

ALTHEA: Oh, "queer" used to mean "strange" or "peculiar," just as "gay" used to mean "happy."

JORDAN: No way!

(PAM enters, finds a notebook on the floor, takes it to JORDAN and ALTHEA. All three read from it.)

PAM: *July 22, 1936. Sometimes I think life is wonderful and sometimes I think it is awful and sometimes I think it is queer.*

JORDAN: *When everything is going along fine and not a thing wrong, something always comes up to ruin it.*

PAM: *And when everything is all wrong and you think you can't stand it another minute, something happens to make things better.*

ALTHEA: *Anything never turns out like you expect it to.*

(PAM laughs in delight at the turn of phrase.)

JORDAN: *When I was little I thought how queer it would be to be sixteen and go with boys.*

PAM: My kids always love this part.

ALTHEA: *But when I did get to sixteen, going with boys just seemed natural.*

JORDAN: *Now I think how queer it will be when I'm in my twenties and married and have children. I guess all that will just seem natural, too, when I get around to it.*

(JORDAN sits on the couch with her feet up. HEATHER enters.)

HEATHER: Let's try these curls again. Well, damn, look how straight it still is.

ALTHEA: I told you it was hopeless. Sometimes I resort to a wig.

JORDAN: Hey, did you know today's my Grandma Pam's birthday?

ALTHEA: Oh, I have a card for her around here somewhere.

JORDAN: She's really old. Fifty-five or something. Oh, sorry.

ALTHEA: When I was your age, fifty-five was really old, too. Thirty was old. And eighty was unthinkably ancient.

HEATHER: Thirty *is* old.

JORDAN: My little sister? She just turned ten and she thought *that* was old.

HEATHER: I thought when I turned thirty I'd finally get the meaning of life. Or at least of my life. Didn't happen.

(PAM enters.)

PAM: Jordan? Are you finished dusting? We've got to get to the store.

(JORDAN resumes dusting, swinging the feather duster.)

You're going to break something.

(JORDAN puts her headphones on, turns the music up loud, exits.)

Give me strength.

ALTHEA: You're very brave to be raising a grandchild in this day and age.

PAM: I think brave is when you have a choice.

ALTHEA: Of course, it's never been easy. My great-grandmother used to walk her children to school with a butcher knife to protect them from the rabid dogs that lurked in the prairie grass.

PAM: Not a lot of rabid dogs around here.

HEATHER: Rabid people, maybe.

ALTHEA: Two of my great-grandparents' four sons were killed in the civil war. The third escaped from a prison camp but he died of fever on his way home. They sent for the fourth son, and he was murdered in the woods by the Cantrell gang for his fine Missouri mules. His father found him hanging from a tree.

HEATHER: Jesus!

PAM: I guess raising kids has always been a risky business.

HEATHER: No shit. And my parents think *I* was hard.

ALTHEA *(TO PAM)*: Do you hear from Jordan's mother?

PAM: Not for a long time. I don't think we will. How did you bear it, Althea?

ALTHEA: That old survival instinct kicks in even when you think you don't want it to.

(JORDAN enters, hands feather duster to PAM who playfully dusts her face with it. JORDAN is not amused.)

PAM *(To ALTHEA)*: Do you want me to straighten up the back bedroom before I go?

ALTHEA: I think Burt's asleep. He was awake most of the night.

HEATHER: Which means you didn't get any sleep, either.

PAM: Not many people would do what you're doing, Althea.

HEATHER: Personally, I don't get it. Why take care of some guy you're not even married to anymore?

ALTHEA: I guess because I can. Being a nurse and all.

HEATHER: Yeah, but you don't have to.

ALTHEA: The thought of him all alone in his apartment in that retirement center, in pain and in his own excrement, just waiting to die, made me feel terrible.

HEATHER: Yeah, that's a bitch. But why is it *your* problem?

ALTHEA: Why not?

PAM: I love you, Althea.

ALTHEA: Oh, I've got a birthday card for you somewhere around here. (*She looks for the card.*)

HEATHER: Well, happy birthday. You're twenty-one, right?

PAM: Actually, I'm fifty-five.

HEATHER: You don't look that old.

PAM: Sure, I do. Which is fine with me.

ALTHEA: More and more, people are calling me "young lady."

"And how are you today, young lady?

Let me help you with that, young lady." As if I ought to be flattered.

HEATHER: Well, yeah, doesn't everybody want to look as young as possible for as long as possible?

PAM: I can't imagine why.

HEATHER: Well, duh. Because young is better than old.

PAM: Why?

(*ALTHEA finds the birthday card, presents it to PAM.*)

ALTHEA: Happy birthday, Pam.

(*PAM reads the card, is moved.*)

PAM: That makes me cry.

HEATHER: Must be a good one.

ALTHEA: Is Richard taking you out dancing as usual?

HEATHER: I wish somebody would take me dancing, birthday or no birthday.

PAM: My husband hates dancing. So taking me once a year for my birthday is a true act of love.

(*JORDAN finds the dancing doll, slips the elastics over her hands and dances a few steps, then puts it down, embarrassed.*)

(to *ALTHEA*): And sometime this week I'll make my birthday pilgrimage to my parents' graves.

ALTHEA: Does it help you to go there? I never did visit Laura's grave very often. Maybe I ought to. But she just isn't there.

HEATHER: God, ladies, such morbid talk!

JORDAN: Really.

ALTHEA: Could you pick me up some bananas while you're

at the store? Burt had the last one for breakfast. Not too green now—I *am* eighty-five, you know.

(PAM and ALTHEA chuckle. JORDAN and HEATHER don't get the joke.)

Oh, and ice cream. Bananas and peach ice cream.

PAM: The essentials!

(PAM and JORDAN exit.)

HEATHER: That girl's got an attitude.

ALTHEA: She's having a hard time, poor thing.

HEATHER: Yeah, well, aren't we all.

ALTHEA: Are you having a hard time, too?

HEATHER: When have you ever known me that I wasn't?

ALTHEA: I'm sure it's not easy being a single mother. I'd like to see Tristan again. I miss having children around.

HEATHER: You want him? You can have him!

ALTHEA: He looks a lot like you did at that age.

HEATHER: I was an ugly little kid.

ALTHEA: You were no such thing!

(HEATHER begins unrolling ALTHEA's hair.)

HEATHER: I was down by the playhouse. This couch used to be in there, didn't it?

ALTHEA: No, this is a different one.

HEATHER: You and your couches.

ALTHEA: I like couches.

HEATHER: When we were kids the only thing Jonathan ever got in trouble for was hiding out there in the playhouse with his nose in some book. Now they pretend like they were proud of it. Maybe *I ought to get some terminal disease and turn into the perfect kid, too.*

ALTHEA: Oh, dear.

HEATHER: Just kidding.

ALTHEA: That poor old playhouse could use some attention, like a lot of things around the place. Somebody called about the basement apartment who says he's handy. I've heard that before, of course, but hope springs eternal.

HEATHER: Didn't you have a renter one time who kept digging up your plants and moving them? Dad used to say,

"Althea's lost her tomatoes again!"

ALTHEA: We had squash vines down the middle of the driveway, and she killed I don't know how many rose bushes. But she did find the perfect spot for the little volunteer peach trees. Whenever I'm picking and canning and eating and giving away all those peaches, I think of her.

HEATHER: Then there was that insane couple from Mississippi that were running a meth lab out of your basement.

ALTHEA: Louisiana.

HEATHER: A meth lab? Really? And who's this guy you've got now?

ALTHEA: He calls me an angel because I let him stay here rent-free. I told him I hereby resign from angelhood. Do you suppose there are support groups for chronic rescuers? He keeps on saying I'm so nice.

HEATHER: You are nice.

ALTHEA: He says it was God's will that he came here. Well, then, I want to know what God has against me!

HEATHER: Keeps your life interesting, anyway.

ALTHEA: One time a friend and I got lost in a blizzard and a nice couple took us in, and we had a perfectly lovely evening. My friend was furious. She said, "I do believe you're *glad* we got in trouble so *you* could meet interesting people." It actually ended our friendship. Isn't that sad?

HEATHER: Althea, this perm's not doing a damn thing for your hair.

ALTHEA: Sometimes I think I'll just shave my head.

(HEATHER combs out ALTHEA's hair.)

HEATHER: Cool. And then paint your scalp. Let's both do it.

ALTHEA: That wouldn't exactly fit the image of the nice little old lady.

HEATHER: My job'd flip out and so would the boyfriend. I think we should do it.

ALTHEA: Your mother and I used to have coffee and chat and she'd brush your hair. It used to just shine in the light through the east window.

HEATHER: And it pulled, and I'd get slapped for not standing still.

ALTHEA: When I said something, your mother would say you had to learn to mind.

HEATHER: I always knew you were on my side.

ALTHEA: I'm still on your side, Heather.

HEATHER: Good thing somebody is.

ALTHEA: What about your boyfriend?

HEATHER: He's on nobody's side but his own.

ALTHEA: Why do you stay with him, then?

HEATHER: Can't think of anything better to do, I guess.

ALTHEA: I hate to hear you talk like that.

HEATHER: You and Mr. Ward always seemed like the perfect couple. *(pause.)* It was a big shock when we realized he wasn't living here anymore. *(pause.)* So, Althea. What happened?

ALTHEA: The oldest story in the book. He left me for another woman.

HEATHER: Mr. Ward? That sweet old man in there?

ALTHEA: You aren't the only one who thought he was sweet. He still has a way with the ladies. When that hospice nurse asked him if there was anything she could do for him and he asked for dancing girls, why, she giggled and said maybe the nurses could dance for him.

HEATHER: Oh, please.

ALTHEA: He said to me once, "the trouble is, sex to you is something holy, and to me it's animal instinct."

HEATHER: That's nice. So the little slut he left you for wasn't the first?

ALTHEA: Nor the last. He left her for someone else, too.

HEATHER: Who'd'a thought.

ALTHEA: He married that one, but he cheated on her too, almost from the very day they got married, and on through her last illness. I know that for a fact.

HEATHER: How do you know that?

ALTHEA: I was there.

HEATHER: What? Oh! Althea Ward!

ALTHEA: You know, I was brought up to feel guilty about so many things, but I never did feel guilty about that. I guess I figured he was my husband, not hers.

HEATHER: You still loved him.

ALTHEA: Some kind of love, I guess. After the divorce we kissed good-bye on the courthouse steps.

HEATHER: I guess you still do love him. I mean, here he is, and you're taking care of him.

ALTHEA: Well, I don't hate him.

HEATHER: I don't know why not. Somebody treated me like that—

(JORDAN and PAM enter with groceries.)

JORDAN: Where do the bananas go?

ALTHEA: In the refrigerator. I think there's room on the bottom shelf.

JORDAN: You can't put bananas in the refrigerator!

ALTHEA: You can if it's your bananas and your refrigerator.

HEATHER: You tell 'em, girlfriend.

(JORDAN rolls her eyes and exits to the kitchen with the bananas.)

HEATHER: So, Althea, what makes a good marriage?

ALTHEA: Oh, dear, you're asking the wrong person. Mama told me if I had any doubts at all about marrying Burt I shouldn't do it.

(JORDAN enters. PAM and JORDAN move to the table.)

PAM: You did have doubts. You wrote about them in your diary.

JORDAN: For posterity.

ALTHEA: When I read those diaries now I want to call back over the years to that foolish young woman—

HEATHER and ALTHEA: "Don't do it!"

(ALTHEA opens a diary. All characters read what she wrote there.)

ALTHEA: *Mama tried to break her engagement to Daddy, but Daddy appealed to Grandma—*

HEATHER: *—he couldn't live without her.*

ALTHEA: *And Grandma told Mama—*

PAM: *—an engagement is almost as sacred a promise as a marriage.*

JORDAN: *So she went ahead with it.*

ALTHEA: *And I don't know as I ever saw a happy or loving moment between them.*

(All but JORDAN look up.)

HEATHER: So what is a good marriage? Not that it makes a lot of difference. I'd probably marry anybody who asked.

PAM: Oh, I suppose agreeing on the important things. Like who cleans the toilet.

JORDAN: Ew.

PAM: So many things go into a good marriage it's a wonder anybody has one.

HEATHER: Hardly anybody does.

PAM: Trust, knowing how to fight fair, shared interests, shared values—

ALTHEA: Good sex.

(Startled laughter from PAM and HEATHER.)

JORDAN: Gross!

HEATHER: You think sex is gross? Oh, honey.

PAM: You just go right on thinking that, okay?

JORDAN: Not sex. Old people's sex.

ALTHEA: I was shocked when it dawned on me that Mama and Daddy must have had relations six times. Only six, because of the twins.

(JORDAN shows ALTHEA a word in the journal she's reading.)

JORDAN: What's that say?

ALTHEA: I think it's "intimate."

HEATHER: So how do you know if you ought to keep trying or just give up and get out?

ALTHEA: When you read about it in your diary fifty years later.

JORDAN: I can't read your writing. *I decided I wasn't going to let him make me*—what's that word?

ALTHEA: Why in the world I wrote in pencil—I think that must be "miserable."

JORDAN: —*miserable forever. I was going to enjoy my life, with him if possible, without him if not.*

HEATHER: I decide that about once a month.

(All read from diaries.)

ALTHEA: *April 22, 1955. If only BURT hadn't waited to start trying in earnest until just about the time I gave up.*

JORDAN: *It wasn't only the affair but afterward when he stayed out late any time he took a notion.*

HEATHER: *He said if I wanted him to stay home I should make it pleasant for him.*

PAM: *Apparently, he had no obligation to make it pleasant for me.*

ALTHEA: *I admit I sometimes took the children to a neighbor's and stayed till bedtime hoping, of course, he'd come home and worry.*

PAM: *If it had been just me, I'd probably have stayed away all night.*

(JORDAN takes the sketch pad and pencils from the toybox and draws.)

HEATHER: *When I heard a car, my hopes and my blood pressure would start rising.*

ALTHEA: *When it went on by, my hopes would fall with a thud and my blood pressure would go on rising.*

PAM: *I'd resolve to be so understanding, charming, gay, loving , and efficient—*efficient?*—that he'd rush home to be every night.*

JORDAN *(drawing)*: This is Antonio. He's the love of my life. He's my soulmate.

HEATHER: *But when he did come, I'd forget all about being loving, understanding, charming, etc., and the whole vicious circle would start over.*

ALTHEA: *He has been trying hard for two years now, and I have, too. Several women have told me how lucky I am to have such a loving, considerate husband.*

PAM: *He tells me he loves me every day.*

JORDAN *(drawing)*: This is Nicholas, the love of my life. He's my soulmate. He's so cool.

HEATHER: *And I say I love him, too, but it doesn't mean much to me.*

ALTHEA: *I thought I knew what love is all about, but I guess I don't anymore. (She closes the journal and the characters move apart.)*

JORDAN *(drawing)*: I can't draw Samantha. She's too beautiful. She's the love of my life. She's my soulmate.

ALTHEA: Is that Burt calling? I guess not. Here I am, trying to figure out a man again, at my age.

HEATHER: Some things never change.

PAM: Some things do, though. If we let them.

HEATHER: Same problems, same hassles, same crap.

PAM: Well, for instance, I'm thinking about quitting.

ALTHEA: Quitting what? You mean teaching?

PAM: Quitting teaching. Wow. That's the first time I've said it out loud.

JORDAN: Why would you do that? You've always been a teacher. That's what you are, except my grandma.

ALTHEA: You love teaching.

PAM: I do. I love it.

HEATHER: What would you do instead?

PAM: I don't know. Yes, actually, I do. There's a book I'd write.

ALTHEA: I remember you gave me one of your stories to read.

PAM: Which you didn't like, because it was fiction.

ALTHEA: I wouldn't say I didn't like it—

PAM: You didn't like it, Althea. You said it wasn't "true."

ALTHEA: Daddy gave me *Little Women* for my eleventh birthday, and I really, truly did use Jo as a role model. Writing a book is a tremendous responsibility, isn't it?

PAM: I write when I can, a little bit here and there. It's always been enough. Now, all of a sudden, it's not.

HEATHER: So do it. Quit. You've got a husband to support you.

PAM: It would be hard for the three of us on just Richard's salary. And I can retire in less than two years.

ALTHEA: Two years isn't very long.

HEATHER: Two years is forever.

JORDAN *(drawing)*: Here's my mom and dad. I look just like them. I don't remember what they look like.

(JORDAN tears out the page, crumples and throws it. PAM starts toward her.)

PAM: Honey—

(JORDAN moves away from her as far as possible. PAM exits. HEATHER stumbles over a toy.)

HEATHER: Shit! That's all I need, Althea, is for you to break a hip because my kid leaves toys all over the place!

(HEATHER throws the toy into the toybox and exits. ALTHEA reads from a journal.)

ALTHEA: *One night when I was four, we got up in the middle of the night and rode for a long time in the wagon.*

(JORDAN turns toward ALTHEA and acts out what she reads.)

Mama hugged me and kissed me and I thought, "What's she doing that for? I'm not going anywhere!" But then I realized they were taking me! They were taking me away from my mother! Later Mama told me that even after we got on the train she could hear me screaming—

JORDAN AND ALTHEA: *Mama! Mama!*

(Downstage spot up on PAM at her parents' graves.)

PAM: "Together in life as in death." But you weren't together very long because, Daddy, you left her. You left me.

(Downstage spot up on HEATHER visiting her brother.)

HEATHER: Hey, little brother, sorry I'm late. Couldn't get away from the kid…he's fine….oh, I'm fine, too, just peachy. How are you?…well, duh, like I don't know that. What, you think "How are you?" is a real question?

(HEATHER and PAM continue in their separate spots, playing separate scenes.)

PAM: Those two years before you died I wasn't allowed to see you for fear I'd get sick, too. I used to stand outside your door. Did you know that, Daddy? But the truth was, I didn't want to see you. *(Pause.)* I'm so sorry.

Althea *(reading from journal)*: *On my first day of kindergarten I was scared, so Aunt Josephine sat with me at one of the little round tables. Then the teacher got me interested in something, and when I looked up Aunt Josephine was gone, without even saying good-bye.*

JORDAN: Good-bye.

HEATHER *(to JONATHAN, whom we do not see)*: Jonathan, it's not fair that you have this stupid disease! Well, shit, then it's not fair that "fair" has nothing to do with it!

PAM: For a long time I was furious that my dad had died of a disease nobody in this country ever got anymore. It just wasn't fair. Now I hear that TB's making a comeback, and I hate to admit it but that makes me feel a little better.

HEATHER: So, the sign said "seeded grapes," and you know how "pitted prunes" means they don't have pits? Well, with grapes apparently that's "seed*less*." Who knew? These have humongous seeds. That's all I need is for you to choke to death—oh, sorry.

PAM: You were a ghost in our house, Daddy. Here I am, twenty-six years older than you were when you died, and you still haunt me.

HEATHER: Oh, for Chrissake, Jonathan, why would you want to "just talk" to me? I've got nothing interesting—did you know that Althea Ward has been keeping a diary for seventy years or something? If I ever wrote in a diary everybody'd die of boredom, even you—oh, God, I'm sorry! So, what do you want to talk about?...Mom and Dad. Why am I not surprised. Give it up, bro. Just because you're—sick doesn't mean we're all gonna love each other....oh, sure, it must be just terribly hard on them, one kid with Aids and the other with shit for a life. My heart bleeds.

(Spot down on HEATHER. HEATHER exits. JORDAN moves to ALTHEA.)

ALTHEA *(reading from another journal)*: *I heard mama calling me in an angry voice and I thought and thought but I couldn't think of anything I'd done to make her mad. I was scared, so I went and hid in the storm cellar. But then I realized—*

Jordan *(reading from the journal)*: *I can't stay down here forever, she'll find me. I might just as well go. And I didn't do anything anyway.*

ALTHEA: *Mama started beating me without saying a word. I was screaming and crying and I fell—*

(JORDAN cowers, covers her head.)

—and she kept on beating me and when the stick broke and a piece of it flew into the stove she got another one and beat me some more.

(JORDAN falls.)

Near the end of her life, the subject of hitting children came up, and I said it might work for some children but it didn't work for me, and she got tears in her eyes and said to me, as if I'd done something wrong, "I can't believe you've held that against me all these years."

(Two beats. JORDAN sits up, arms still over her head.)

PAM: You were certainly not a ghost, Mom. You were about as real as it gets. We did have our share of knock-down-drag-outs, didn't we? I'd see you'd been crying and I feel guilty that I didn't feel guilty.

(JORDAN gets the dancing doll out of the toybox. ALTHEA reads from another journal.)

ALTHEA: *Mother's day, 1987. I woke up to the sound of Mama's labored breathing. I took her pulse and it was steady. She took one or two more breaths and was still. I listened to her heart with a stetho-scope and for a minute or two I could hear its weak beating. Then it was still, too.*

(Pause. Then HEATHER enters, shows JORDAN how to dance with the doll.)

PAM: You always had the answers. That's what mothers are supposed to do, right?

ALTHEA: *I sang some of her favorite hymns.*

(HEATHER and JORDAN softly sing a hymn behind ALTHEA's next speech.)

I brushed and braided her hair, crying all the while. Her face looked so peaceful with all the lines smoothed out.

PAM: Me, I'd get almost paralyzed by all the day-to-day decisions. She's been fed and changed and held, so why is she still screaming? How can she hate school when both her parents are teachers? Is her moodiness from drugs or just adolescence?

ALTHEA: *For the funeral I suggested the lavender suit and lacy white blouse she'd worn for her 100th birthday party. But Georgia picked out the old brown dress with white polka dots.*

(HEATHER and JORDAN fight over the doll, saying lines as if from the argument between ALTHEA and her sister.)

HEATHER: This was her favorite dress! She was always wearing it!

JORDAN: Yeah, around the house. She wouldn't wear it in public.

ALTHEA: *Then, incredibly, I said, "She wouldn't have been caught dead in it!"*

(HEATHER and JORDAN exit, leaving the doll on the couch.)

PAM: Didn't you ever have any doubts about anything, mom? Not even about your painting? You were good, you know. Those two landscapes in the living room and the portrait of daddy I found wrapped in a sheet in the back of the closet—did you know I found that one? But you gave it up, to tend to daily life. To tend to me. How could you do that? I've never for-given you.

ALTHEA: I've come to think that being a parent is more than should be asked of any human being.

(Lights down on ALTHEA and PAM. JORDAN enters and exits several times carrying garage sale items.)

PAM: God help us, you've been to a garage sale.

(ALTHEA enters carrying an armload of clothes.)

ALTHEA: Jordan dear, would you mind helping Heather get the couch off the top of the car?

PAM: Couch?

ALTHEA: They were throwing away a perfectly good couch. I like couches.

(ALTHEA sits with the clothes in her lap. PAM, HEATHER, and JORDAN make several trips to bring in other items, which remain onstage throughout the rest of the play. JORDAN stealthily sets aside a suitcase from among the items.)

(to BURT who is unseen, offstage in his room) Burt, you're awake...excuse me, but I do believe that at this stage of my life I can have as many couches as I want...."sit a while," I have to find someplace to put all these rescued items. The new couch can go on the porch. Let me go, Burt.

(ALTHEA sits at table, writes in journal. Pause. JORDAN enters.)

Jordan, how about some ice cream?

JORDAN: Ice cream? In the morning?

ALTHEA: Last night I had oatmeal for supper. Today I had turkey with all the trimmings for breakfast. Life is full of little adventures. It's my favorite—peach.

(ALTHEA exits. JORDAN picks up the doll, dances, then hastily puts it down when ALTHEA enters.)

Isn't that a nice doll?

JORDAN: I was just looking at it.

ALTHEA: Would you mind holding these a minute?

(ALTHEA gives the bowls of ice cream to JORDAN, executes a few dance steps with the doll.)

(TO BURT) Oh, Burt, for heaven's sake. I was just dancing....I get so tired of being careful!...Well, would *you* like some ice cream? I do believe ice cream tastes best for breakfast...No? Are you sure?

JORDAN: What's his problem? He's not the boss of you.

ALTHEA: Ah, but he would dearly love to be. I was just reading about that in my journal, in fact.

(ALTHEA finds the right journal and the right passage as PAM and HEATHER enter. All three read from the same journal.)

June 15, 1944. This morning when I went for the milk, little Shirley wanted to run down to the river and back, so we did, just to be running. I felt young and wild and free. Shirley said:

JORDAN: *Let's run away!*

ALTHEA: *And I said:*

HEATHER: *How about if you run away from your mother and I run away from my baby?*

ALTHEA: *How fun it is to do and say childish things when you're an adult and in no danger of punishment!* Burt, if you'd been there, you'd have said:

ALTHEA and JORDAN: "Althea, whatever am I going to do with you?"

ALTHEA: And I'd have said back:

Althea and HEATHER: "Whatever would you do without me?"

(JORDAN brings the doll to ALTHEA.)

JORDAN: Was this doll your daughter's? The one that got—

PAM: Jordan.

ALTHEA: It's okay to say it, dear. If she could go through it, I can certainly hear the word. She was murdered. That's the truth of it.

PAM: Oh, Althea.

ALTHEA: No, Mama made that doll for me, and I didn't even have to share her.

JORDAN: I thought your mom was mean to you.

ALTHEA: The other day I came across a letter she wrote me when I was in training and so terribly lonely that started, "Dearest darling Althea-girl."

PAM: That's nice.

ALTHEA: And once when Burt was being very critical of me, as usual, she spoke up. "Now you listen here, I love Althea more than anything in the world and I want you to stop treating her that way!"

JORDAN: But she beat you. For no reason.

ALTHEA: Yes. Yes, she did.

JORDAN: Grandma Pam told me you had to take care of her

for a long time when she got old.

ALTHEA: Just like she took care of her mother. She'd say, "It was my *duty!*"

JORDAN: No way am I ever doing that.

PAM: Just what your grandpa and I like to hear.

ALTHEA (*reading from journal*): *August 10, 1965. Today's BURT's brother called to tell him their father was very sick and he should go see him right away. On the phone BURT sounded congenial and concerned.*

(*HEATHER acts out the scene.*)

HEATHER: *Why, sure, I will. I'll go right after work. He's my dad. I owe him a lot. You bet.*

ALTHEA: *But when he hung up and turned back to us, it was an altogether different story. We knew he hated his father.*

HEATHER: *Why doesn't that old man just die and get it over with?*

ALTHEA: *BURT was—and is—a person of strong and often conflicting emotions. He loved his children but was jealous if them, valued our life together but at times wanted no part of it. He told me once:*

HEATHER: *This is what I've always dreamed of. But there's a part of me that doesn't give a damn about my dreams.*

JORDAN (*looking through journals*): Who's Gary Davis? Isn't he that murderer dude?

ALTHEA: He was on death row for fifteen years before he was executed.

JORDAN: Why would you want to write to a murderer?

ALTHEA: Somebody in citizens against capital punishment—or maybe it was murder victims' families for reconciliation—anyway, somebody gave me his address and said he'd appreciate a letter. I just couldn't imagine what it must be like to live on death row.

JORDAN: Did you feel sorry for him or something? I wouldn't feel sorry for him.

ALTHEA: I guess I wanted to understand the human mind that would be capable of doing such a terrible thing.

JORDAN: And do you?

ALTHEA: Do I understand him? Do I understand why Laura died? No.

JORDAN: Omigod, was Gary Davis the one that killed—

PAM: Jordan.

ALTHEA: No, he murdered somebody else's daughter. The man who killed my daughter was executed, too, though not for her murder.

JORDAN: I bet you were happy.

HEATHER: I'd have been partying.

ALTHEA: People did. But I wasn't happy. I had a very disturbing dream. I wrote about it. I wrote in my diary a great deal then.

(All characters read from ALTHEA's journals.)

PAM: Here's a passage that always meant a lot to me, and to my kids, too. Annie could still recite it, a generation later. *(Pam reads from journal.)*

When my strength and courage aren't equal to the struggle, I remember a saying from the knights of old.

JORDAN *(reading from journal)*: *I lay me down and bleed a while, then rise and fight again.*

HEATHER *(reading from journal)*: *My way of bleeding a while is to sort out my thoughts by writing in my journal. Then I feel my strength returning and I'm ready to cope as best I can.*

ALTHEA *(reading from another journal)*: *Dear Gary Davis, I saw you on tv last night. I saw how young you are, and how handsome. You are the same age as my oldest son, and I thought how I would feel if he were in your place. That made me feel closer to you.*

JORDAN: Gross.

ALTHEA: I even signed it, "Love, Althea Ward."

JORDAN: Well, I hope my mom and dad are dead.

ALTHEA: Oh, dear.

PAM: You're talking about my daughter.

JORDAN: If I ever get the chance I'll fuckin' off 'em myself!

(JORDAN throws journals and loose pages across the stage, exits.)

ALTHEA: Oh, dear.

PAM: I'm sorry, Althea.

(PAM exits after JORDAN. HEATHER gathers the scattered journals as ALTHEA, not much fazed, continues to read.)

ALTHEA: *It was such a strange, vivid dream. I dreamed I was awakened before dawn by a pounding at the door.*

(Loud knocking far offstage. PAM enters and acts out the scene.)
PAM: *Let me in! Please! Let me in!*
(JORDAN enters and acts out the scene.)
JORDAN: Hide me!
(HEATHER acts out the scene.)
HEATHER: *They're gonna kill me!*
ALTHEA: *We were out there in the yard, and a shadowy figure appeared, and I knew it was Laura. Then all of a sudden the police came and they took him. And there was a big hole with water in it and slime in the bottom, and one of the policemen said to this poor, frightened young man:*
HEATHER: *If you'd just get down there in that hole, you'd save us a lot of work.*
ALTHEA: *And they were going to shoot him right there. I put my arms around him and Laura put her arms around us both.*
(All hug themselves.)
And I cried out to them:
PAM: *Can't you at least give him a tranquilizer?*
JORDAN: *Then I woke up.*
ALTHEA: *It was the day Laura's murderer was to be executed. I looked at the clock and at first I thought it was a couple of hours yet, but then I remembered about the time difference and I knew it was exactly the time. And I couldn't stop crying.*
(They move toward each other as they cry out.)
Laura!
PAM: Daddy!
HEATHER: Jonathan!
JORDAN: Mom!
(HEATHER moves to downstage spot and speaks to TRISTAN, whom we do not see.)
HEATHER: You're mama's little man, aren't you Tristan? Tristan, are you Mama's little man? I'd sing to you if I knew any lullabies.
(Pause. Then HEATHER begins singing "99 Bottles of Beer int he Wall" as a lullaby, continues singing as ALTHEA moves toward BURT's bedroom door.)
ALTHEA: Oh, well, Burt, no, I guess I don't mind if you hold my hand. I guess I could sit for a few minutes.

(PAM joins HEATHER and begins to sing a real lullaby. After a moment, HEATHER joins in. They continue singing softly behind ALTHEA's next lines.)

No, I will not kiss you. No, Burt, I won't.

(PAM and HEATHER stop singing as doorbell rings. ALTHEA exits to answer it.)

Heather *(to TRISTAN)*: Stop saying, "Mommy!" You're making me crazy!

PAM: Before I had kids I longed for somebody to call me "Mommy." After I had kids there were days when I thought I'd scream if I heard it one more time.

HEATHER: Tell me about it. No matter what I do for him it's not enough.

PAM: The last time I talked to Jordan's mother on the phone, she called me Mommy.

HEATHER: Goddammit, what do you *want*? Stop it! Stop saying Mommy!

(PAM, HEATHER, and JORDAN speak not quite in unison.)

JORDAN *(cradling the dancing doll)*: Mommy!

HEATHER *(pantomiming holding TRISTAN)*: Mommy!

PAM *(echoing her daughter on the phone)*: Mommy!

(ALTHEA enters, sits, looks through journals.)

ALTHEA *(reading from journal)*: *April 18, 1940. My dear little sister, you were eighteen day before yesterday, but I would still like to tell you some things about the decision you are considering.*

JORDAN *(to PAM)*: I don't *know*, grandma! God! Careers are stupid. I'll just get some job.

PAM: Isn't there anything that interests you?

JORDAN: Just because *you're* a teacher!

HEATHER: All jobs suck. Like at my stupid-ass hotel the other day, some lady threw a total fit because we don't have grits on the menu. And they said I had to give her a full refund. Grits!

ALTHEA *(reading)*: *In our first-year ethics book it said, the work of a nurse—"*

PAM: The work of a teacher—

ALTHEA and PAM: *"—will cause her to become either noble or callous."*

ALTHEA: *I found this quite daunting, as I didn't want to be callous and I didn't think I could be noble. But there is truth in it. The work is fascinating, maddening, degrading, uplifting—*

PAM: *—tiresome, and soul-satisfying. It brings out the best and the worst.*

JORDAN: Sick people suck. Little kids suck. Maybe I'll be a rock star. *(JORDAN plays air guitar.)*

PAM *(eagerly)*: Maybe you'd like music lessons again?

JORDAN: I suck at music.

PAM: You were first-chair flute.

JORDAN: No! Stop hassling me.

ALTHEA: *The work brings headaches, footaches, and heartaches. The deep satisfaction of knowing you did your best and the deep guilt of knowing you didn't.*

PAM *(to JORDAN)*: You're really good at art.

JORDAN: You leave my art out of this. That's mine.

PAM: Don't waste your talent, Jordan.

JORDAN: It's mine. I can waste it if I want to.

PAM: Don't neglect what feeds your soul.

JORDAN *(mocking)*: Feeds my soul?

PAM: That's what my mother did.

JORDAN: I know. You told me. She was this fantastic artist and she quit because she had to take care of you and she always said she'd do it later, but she never did. Yeah, well, I'm not her.

PAM: Your mother had, has, some talent. It broke your grandpa's heart when she stopped—

JORDAN: Shut up!

PAM *(mildly)*: Careful.

JORDAN: Sorry, grandma. *(JORDAN leafs through one of the journals.)*

Listen to this. This is so weird. *July 10, 1953. Laura kept squirming and crossing her legs, all the time insisting she didn't have to go. Finally, she dashed to the bathroom, and I thought it might teach her a lesson if she wet her pants.*

(HEATHER acts out the scene.)

HEATHER: Mama! I made it!

PAM *(reading from the journal)*: *This must have been the age-old impulse to go as close as possible to the edge of a cliff without falling off.*

HEATHER: Boy, I hear that!

JORDAN *(to Pam)*: Well, see ya later. *(JORDAN starts to exit.)*

PAM: Hold on. Where are you going?

JORDAN: Out.

PAM: Out where and with whom?

JORDAN: To a movie, and with Brittany. Okay?

PAM: See you by 11:00.

(JORDAN exits. PAM looks after her for a moment, then exits opposite.)

HEATHER: Althea, can I stay here for a while?

ALTHEA: Of course you may, but what's wrong? What about Tristan?

HEATHER: He's better off with his dad.

ALTHEA: A child needs his mother—

HEATHER: Please, Althea, I don't really have anywhere else to go.

ALTHEA: Maybe you could help me with Burt.

HEATHER: Sure, I guess. I don't know anything—

ALTHEA: I was just going to turn him.

(HEATHER and ALTHEA exit to BURT's room. JORDAN enters opposite, sneaks ALTHEA's journals and papers into the suitcase from the garage sale, checks the address on an envelope from her pocket, exits quickly.)

HEATHER *(offstage)*: Holy shit!

ALTHEA *(offstage)*: Burt! What have you done?

Lights down.

ACT II

The next day. Lights up as ALTHEA enters from BURT's room, talking to him over her shoulder.

ALTHEA: Well, yes, Burt, I imagine it does pain you. You didn't hit anything critical, but you managed to wound yourself. And, I might add, make quite a mess for other people to clean up....it's a little late for "sorry," don't you think? Altogether too late for "sorry." And I have other things on my mind just now. For one thing, Jordan's missing. Remember when Laura was missing? It started with just one night, like this.

(HEATHER trips over TRISTAN's toys, angrily kicks them out of the way, then tenderly picks them up and holds them close.)

(Still to BURT, though no longer looking in his direction)

A lot of my diaries are missing, too....oh, Burt, for heaven's sake, I wouldn't have misplaced all that....well, it may seem foolish to you, but I've always had the sneaking suspicion that things weren't real unless I wrote them down.

HEATHER: Did you write anything in there about how to be a good mother? I really want to be a good mother.

ALTHEA: Worrying about being a good mother is part of being a good mother, I think.

HEATHER: It's so hard. I can't even take care of myself—how can I take care of somebody else? How can I show a kid how to live when I don't have a clue? I need online help or something.

ALTHEA: My grandmother spent years writing the story of her life, and then it was destroyed in a fire. So she started all over from the beginning. She wrote something in there about what it was like raising children in her day.

HEATHER: Could I read it sometime?

ALTHEA: Of course. Pam liked it. I thought Jordan might, too, but she hasn't seemed—oh, dear, I do hope she's all right.

HEATHER: I ran away all the time and nothing bad happened to me. Well, nothing really bad. Hey, you know what? I bet she's the one stole your journals.

ALTHEA: Whatever for?

HEATHER: Just to be mean, jerk you around.

ALTHEA: Jordan wouldn't—

HEATHER: Or maybe to see how you've lived your life so she can figure out how she's supposed to live hers. That makes sense.

ALTHEA: That's flattering, dear, but I think I know less now than I did when I was her age.

HEATHER: Yeah, but you've been there. Maybe not the exact same thing she's going through or I'm going through, but it's *about* the same stuff, you know? Themes or something?

ALTHEA *(looking around)*: I've been saving a lovely blank book for a special occasion, but now I can't find it. So I guess I'll just write on any old paper, just as I've always done.

(ALTHEA reads as she writes, beginning with the actual date of the performance.)

(Date of performance.) I have in mind to record thoughts and feelings and observations for posterity, and also, in a queer way, for generations who've gone before.

HEATHER *(reading)*: Sometimes I think of my diaries as the damning evidence of my many mistakes, and I have a strong urge to burn them all.

(to ALTHEA) See? That's why I don't write down what I think or do or dream or whatever. It'd just sound stupid.

ALTHEA *(reading)*: That would be admitting that I've wasted my life and now I'm too old and tired to redeem myself. But who in the world will care about all these unremarkable observations about an unremarkable little life?

HEATHER: I will. *(Beat.)*

ALTHEA: Why, thank you, dear. *(beat.)* I'm hungry. Are you hungry?

HEATHER: Not really.

ALTHEA *(exiting to kitchen)*: I'll be right back.

(HEATHER dials her cell phone, gets a busy signal.)

HEATHER *(hanging up impatiently)*: Jonathan, get off the damn phone, or out of the chat room. I need to talk to you.

(ALTHEA enters, singing "You'd be so nice to come home to.")

That's a pretty song.

ALTHEA: Burt used to sing it to me when we were first married.

HEATHER: So why'd he quit?

ALTHEA: I don't rightly know. I guess he didn't mean it anymore.

HEATHER: People say all kinds of crap they don't mean.

ALTHEA: I think he might have meant it. For that moment.

HEATHER: Come to think of it, I say all kinds of crap I don't really mean.

ALTHEA: Burt and I used to brush each other's hair.

HEATHER *(shudders)*: Ew, I would hate that.

ALTHEA: It was nice.

HEATHER *(noticing ALTHEA is eating something)*: Is that

the cake that's been in the frig for a hundred years? I thought I threw it out.

(During the following exchange, PAM enters, looks through JORDAN's sketchbook.)

ALTHEA: There's not a thing wrong with this cake. Maybe it's a little dry, but it isn't moldy. I'm planning on having it for breakfast.

HEATHER: You can't eat that. We need to throw it away.

ALTHEA: Good heavens, you sound like a parent with a stubborn child.

HEATHER: Come on, Althea, give it to me.

(ALTHEA gobbles the cake.)

ALTHEA: Too late! Ha!

HEATHER: You are one stubborn old lady, you know that?

ALTHEA: Thank you.

PAM: If there are any clues in here about where Jordan is, they escape me.

ALTHEA: You haven't had any word?

PAM: Richard's out searching while I make phone calls. We know the drill. I really don't want to be doing this again.

ALTHEA: Do you have any idea at all where she might have gone?

PAM: She got a birthday card from her mother—six weeks late—and there was a return address on the envelope. Like an idiot, I didn't write it down.

ALTHEA: Oh, dear.

PAM: Or, she might just be out partying.

ALTHEA: Didn't she do this before.

PAM: She's never been gone overnight before.

ALTHEA: I bet things will turn out all right. I never did run away, though I wanted to. Did you?

PAM: In eighth grade study hall my best friend and I used to write these long letters to each other about how we'd run off to Mexico and live on the beach with our boyfriends. We wouldn't have any money, but we'd have our love. So romantic. So passionate.

HEATHER: So dumb.

PAM: I knew it was dumb. I don't think either my daughter

or my granddaughter gets that.

HEATHER: Ever since I was about twelve I think I've spent more time running than I have at home. I'm still doing that.

PAM: *(looking through the sketchbook):* There are some portraits in here of people I don't know. Of course, they could just be made up.

(HEATHER looks at the sketches.)

HEATHER: Hey, those are pretty good.

PAM: Jordan has a lot of talents. Which she does everything in her power to waste.

HEATHER *(reading from the sketchbook):* "Antonio, the love of my life. Nicholas, the love of my life. Samantha, the love of my life." She's bi?

PAM: Apparently it's trendy among girls her age.

ALTHEA: Bisexual, you mean? Really?

HEATHER: I am definitely not bi! No, thank you. Just men are more trouble than they're worth.

PAM: That's a great message to give your son.

HEATHER: Oh, lighten up.

(Carrying the toys, HEATHER moves downstage for a monologue. She is speaking to TRISTAN, who is offstage toward the audience.)

Hey, Tristan, look what I found. Wanna play trucks with me?....oh, come on. You can watch TV at your dad's.

(HEATHER puts the toys down, attaches the dancing doll to her feet, dances.)

Look at this great doll, Tristan! Althea's mommy made it for her a long time ago....well, sure, Althea had a mommy. Everybody has a mommy....you pay attention to me, dammit! I'm your mother! Do you hear me?

(HEATHER tosses the doll onto the couch.)

PAM: I don't suppose you know where my granddaughter is?

HEATHER: Haven't seen her.

PAM: And she didn't say anything to you?

HEATHER: It's not like we're buds.

PAM: You'd tell me, right?

HEATHER: Can't say. Girls just wanna have fun, you know?

PAM: Althea, you'd tell me if you knew anything, wouldn't

you? You wouldn't decide she's some sort of free spirit and we should let her do what she wants?

ALTHEA: Of course I'd tell you, dear. Probably.

PAM: Probably?

ALTHEA: Honestly, Pam, I don't know anything. I'm afraid I've been preoccupied with Burt—

PAM: Oh, I didn't even ask. I'm sorry. How is he?

(HEATHER makes call on her cell phone.)

ALTHEA: He has quite a lot of pain. But we don't think there's serious damage. He won't go to a doctor.

PAM: I wouldn't think it would be easy to stab yourself.

ALTHEA: He says now he knows what the word "leatherneck" means.

HEATHER: What *does* it mean?

(To JONATHAN on the phone) Hey, little bro, how's it hangin'? Don't answer that...don't answer that! I'm your sister!

PAM *(to ALTHEA)*: Does he say why he did it?

ALTHEA: He says his hunting knife went off while he was cleaning it.

PAM: What?

ALTHEA: That's what he says.

Heather *(to JONATHAN on the phone)*: Oh, crappy day at work. What else is new.

ALTHEA: I suppose he did it because he was just tired.

HEATHER *(to JONATHAN on the phone)*: If you want to know the truth I'm feeling a little—I don't know, desperate at the moment. My life just keeps getting suckier, know what I'm sayin'?

ALTHEA *(to PAM)*: Tired and desperate, I'd guess.

HEATHER *(to JONATHAN on the phone)*: This fancy-ass bitch in her little business suit with her little briefcase doing some kind of fancy-ass deal on her cell phone, she just went off on me because the tv in her room had a white line across the screen. Went *off.*

PAM *(to ALTHEA)*: Can I help you with him before I go?

HEATHER *(to JONATHAN on the phone)*: Called me an incompetent little bitch. It was the "little" that totally pissed me off.

ALTHEA *(to PAM)*: I dressed the wounds this morning, and hospice will be here soon.

HEATHER *(to JONATHAN on the phone)*: So they fired me.

(Calling.) Tristan, Mommy will be off the phone in a minute!

PAM *(to ALTHEA)*: Are you okay?

ALTHEA: I'm sad, and I'm mad. Mostly sad.

HEATHER *(to JONATHAN on the phone)*: Look, Jonathan, can I move in with you? I could take care of you. We could take care of each other, you know?

PAM *(to ALTHEA)*: I better go.

ALTHEA: Do the police still insist a missing person isn't missing until they've been missing twenty-four hours? If we'd been able to file a report on Laura that first day, I always thought maybe—

HEATHER *(to JONATHAN on the phone)*: No, it's fine, don't worry about it. I hear you.

PAM *(to ALTHEA)*: They say most runaways come home on their own.

ALTHEA: That's what they said about—

PAM *(hastily)*: I better go.

(PAM exits.)

ALTHEA: That's what they said about Laura.

HEATHER *(to TRISTAN)*: What, Tristan?

(To JONATHAN on the phone): I'm gonna have to call you back. *(HEATHER hangs up.)*

(Glaring at the phone): Not any time soon.

(Spot up downstage far right on JORDAN; set suggests the playhouse. She is writing in ALTHEA's missing fancy blank book. At first she reads as she is writing, then stops writing and just tells her dream. The other characters enter, stand around her at the edge of her spot, act out what she tells. This dream sequence should echo ALTHEA's as much as possible.)

JORDAN: I fell asleep on the couch in the playhouse and I had this weird dream. I dreamed I went everywhere and I couldn't find my mom and dad, and then I found them but I couldn't remember what they looked like so I didn't know if it was really them or not, but then they called me—

PAM: Jordan? Jordan?

HEATHER: Yo! Jordan!

JORDAN: —and then I knew it was them and I ran after them, and they disappeared inside this creepy house and I tried to go after them but I couldn't find the door and then I did but it was locked.

(Knocking offstage.)

ALTHEA: Let me in! Please let me in!

JORDAN: Then this shadowy figure just kind of appeared and I knew it was—

ALTHEA: —Laura!

JORDAN: I don't know what she was doing in my dream. Maybe because I think she'd have been a good mother. I think about her a lot, like what if she was my mother and she was murdered?

HEATHER: Oh, you mean instead of just running off and leaving you?

JORDAN: And then there was this big hole with water in it and slime on the bottom and my mom and dad were on one side of it and I was on the other side and I said—oh, God, I said—

HEATHER: If you'd just get down there in that hole—

JORDAN *(crying)*: —you'd save me a lot of hassle.

ALTHEA: Mom and Dad put their arms around each other.

PAM: And I put my arms around them both.

JORDAN: And then I woke up.

(ALTHEA, PAM, and HEATHER move out of the light. Spot stays up on JORDAN for a moment. Spot down. JORDAN exits. Lights up on HEATHER in the same place as just before the dream sequence.)

HEATHER *(to TRISTAN)*: Tristan. What do you want from me? Are you trying to make me crazy?

ALTHEA: I wrote about feeling like that when my children were small. Oh, I do wish I had it! Maybe I can remember—it would have been about '46 or '47, in the fall, so let's say *October 10, 1946. Often I don't feel like ALTHEA, only BURT's wife and my children's mother.*

HEATHER: He just never stops! He's always wanting a piece of me. Like some goddamn little mosquito.

ALTHEA: *Then it seems they're misbehaving purposely to annoy me. And the baby is just a busy little nuisance, pulling lamps over, splashing in the toilet, turning over the garbage.*

HEATHER: I know he's just doing it to get on my nerves.

ALTHEA: *And BURT is just a guy who comes home and asks, "Isn't dinner ready yet?" Or, "Son, do you suppose we could talk your mama into sewing some buttons on these pajamas?" Or "When are you going to darn my socks?"*

HEATHER: You darned his socks?

ALTHEA: Not often enough, to hear him tell it.

HEATHER: Would you mind keeping Tristan busy for a few minutes while I call my brother back? We're having sort of a fight.

ALTHEA: How's he doing?

HEATHER: Hell if I know. We never got that far because Tristan kept bugging me.

ALTHEA *(to TRISTAN)*: Tristan, would you like to hear a poem my children loved when they were your age? I bet I still know it by heart...Mommy's busy right now.

HEATHER *(to TRISTAN)*: You sure he won't bother you? Tristan, don't you bother Althea.

ALTHEA: It's nice having a child around.

(HEATHER makes a call on her cell phone.)

Beautiful bountiful Janet Jeannette

Was both kith and kin to the queen of Tibet

Was charming in every conceivable way

Till the wizard Wakworian stole her away.

HEATHER *(to JONATHAN on the phone)*: Hey. I can talk for a few minutes.....Althea's watching him. She's always taking over. I mean, he's my kid, not hers.

ALTHEA:

Janet Jeannette, who was kith to the queen

Was the prettiest kith that had ever been seen

And the strongest and smartest of anyone's kin

Whom wizard Wakworian wanted to win.

HEATHER *(to JONATHAN on the phone)*: You're probably right. You always are. I guess I'll just stay here for a while. She needs me.

ALTHEA: I always thought somebody ought to ask the fair maiden what *she* wanted.

HEATHER *(to JONATHAN on the phone)*: Well, little bro, guess I better go spend quality time with the kid. Later. *(HEATHER hangs up.)*

Shit.

(to TRISTAN) hey, Tristan, I thought you wanted to go to the park with me. If you're not too *busy*.

ALTHEA: How's Jonathan?

HEATHER: Hell if I know. He doesn't tell me anything, always gets me talking about myself. Tristan, you ready? We'll go to the park for a little while and then I'll take you home.

ALTHEA: Wasn't his father going to pick him up here?

HEATHER: Yeah. He jerks me around all the time, let's see how he likes it. Just tell him I took him to his house. *(HEATHER exits.)*

ALTHEA: Bye, Tristan. Come see me again.

(ALTHEA finds a letter under the table near BURT's room.)

(To BURT) Well, Burt, here's a letter I wrote to you that you never answered. It must have fallen out when whoever it was took my journals. Who would want my journals? Anyway, I guess I kept a copy of this, for posterity. Or as evidence.

(ALTHEA reads.)

February 1, 1965. You say you can't talk to me, so perhaps you can write. I'm saying this for the last time: We have already ruined what should have been the best years of our lives. Let's try to salvage what we have left. If you have any suggestions at all, I will follow them. If your attitude is still that we have no choice but to live together in hostility, I will have to make my own decisions.

(To BURT) the least you could have done was answer. How about giving me an answer now?

(Seeing that BURT has fallen asleep, ALTHEA gives up. HEATHER enters, carrying a journal.)

HEATHER: Is this yours? *(HEATHER hands the journal to ALTHEA.)*

ALTHEA: My diary from 1975. The year Laura died. Where'd you find it?

HEATHER: On the doorstep.

ALTHEA: Oh, do you think Jordan put it there? I better call Pampo.

HEATHER: Be sure she knows I had nothing to do with it.

(ALTHEA exits. HEATHER reads aloud from the journal. ALTHEA enters while HEATHER is reading.)

January 4, 1975. Today Mama and I took the decorations off the tree. She said, "I wonder who will be gone by next Christmas?" I'm sure thoughts like that come naturally when you're eighty-five years old.

(To ALTHEA) Everything you write is so deep and meaningful and interesting. How do you do that? I could never do that.

ALTHEA: I don't know about that, but at least it's honest as to how I see things at the time. I mean, if you put up a front in a diary, of all places, you'd have to be pretty far gone.

HEATHER: Could you teach me how to do that?

ALTHEA: I did take a journal-writing class one time, but I never could see that there was much to learn. You just record what you feel and what you observe, as faithfully as you can.

HEATHER: Yeah, but I wouldn't know faithful and honest if they bit me in the ass.

ALTHEA: It just takes a little practice.

HEATHER: What if I wrote to you instead of just to myself, and you could tell me if it's honest and faithful.

ALTHEA: Oh, dear. How would I know?

HEATHER: You'd know better than me. And then you could write in your diary and pretend you were writing back to me.

ALTHEA: Why? Are you going somewhere?

HEATHER: I'm no good to anybody around here.

ALTHEA: What about your son?

HEATHER: Will you keep my letters for him when he's older? And copies of the ones you write to me?

ALTHEA: Don't do this, Heather. He needs you. So does your brother.

HEATHER: I thought maybe Jonathan needed me because he was dying. But he could live like this for years, and he's got more friends than he has time for, and our parents visit him every day. What's left for me to do?

ALTHEA: Just be there. Just love them. Sometimes that's all we can do. Sometimes it's no small thing.

HEATHER *(angry, crying)*: I don't know about love! Love's

supposed to be Jonathan's thing! My thing is fear. *(HEATHER exits.)*

ALTHEA: Oh, dear.

(Pause. ALTHEA exits to check on BURT. JORDAN enters, lays a journal open on the floor with a drawing beside it, hurriedly exits. ALTHEA enters, doesn't see the journal and drawing. She stops and turns to talk to BURT.)

Well, Burt, it's getting late. Is there anything I can do for you before I have my last banana of the day and go to bed?

(Coyly) What do you mean, "Say good-night sweetly"?...oh, I know very well what you mean. All right, I will, I will say good-night sweetly.

(Teasing) Good-night sweetly!

(Giggling, ALTHEA exits opposite, returns with a banana from the refrigerator, sees the journal and drawing, retrieves them.)

Why, here's one of my missing journals. And a drawing—Jordan?

(ALTHEA looks for JORDAN, then opens the journal and reads.)

August 25, 1975, neighbors came with a big pot of chili and spice cake and a blue bowl of fresh peaches. Then, oddly, I felt as if I had to do some cleaning. My vacuum is being repaired so I went to borrow one. Mrs. Monroe came to the door still in her nightgown and I knew something was wrong even before she said, "my sister died, I just got back last night." I told her about Laura, and we held each other and cried and she said, "ALTHEA, ALTHEA, what is to become of us?"

(PAM enters hurriedly.)

PAM: Is she here?

ALTHEA: I don't know where she is, but I think she left this.

(ALTHEA shows PAM the journal and drawing.)

PAM: But what is it? Does it mean something?

ALTHEA *(pointing with the banana)*: It sort of looks like a face, don't you think? There's the mouth, and that could be an eye.

PAM: Or it could be a bowl of ice cream for all I know. When did you find this?

ALTHEA: Just now.

PAM: Could she have been hiding somewhere in your house all this time?

ALTHEA: Oh, dear. One time the police came looking for a

renter and they didn't find her because she was under my bed! I don't think they ever did believe me that I didn't know.

PAM: Is it okay if I look around?

ALTHEA: Maybe you should look under my bed.

PAM (*starts to exit, stops*): I meant to tell you—your neighbor Mrs. Monroe? She came running over just as I pulled into the driveway—well, not exactly running, but hurrying. She took me by the shoulders and got right up in my face and sort of shook me a little and she whispered, "that Althea ward is going to go to heaven with her shoes on!" (*pause.*) What does that mean?

ALTHEA: I have no idea. But I rather like the sound of it.

(*PAM exits hurriedly. ALTHEA lays the banana on the table, finds the notebook she is now using as a journal, sits and writes. During the following scene, JORDAN enters stealthily, steals the banana, exits. Absorbed in her writing, ALTHEA doesn't notice. PAM and HEATHER enter.*)

PAM: Heather, are you sure you don't know anything about Jordan?

HEATHER: You know what? I've got other things on my mind besides your crazy granddaughter.

PAM: I'm sure you do.

HEATHER: What's that supposed to mean?

PAM: Nothing. It means nothing. Right now, nothing means anything except Jordan—oh, the basement! Maybe she's down there.

HEATHER: I'll look around outside.

(*HEATHER and PAM exit.*)

ALTHEA (*looking around*): Now, I know I had a banana. I put it right here where I'd know where it was.

(*To BURT, teasing*) Burt, did you get up out of that bed and sneak out here and steal my banana? I just bet you did. Well, I'm coming in there and reclaiming it!

(*ALTHEA stops at BURT's door. Pause.*) Burt? Oh, dear.

(*ALTHEA exits into BURT's room. Pause. ALTHEA enters, writes in her journal.*)

Burt is dying.

(*ALTHEA shakes her head, closes the journal and holds it close, returns to look in at BURT.*) Burt is dying, right here and now.

(To BURT) I'm glad it's almost over for you, Burt....your face is so gaunt, but still handsome, and still with those expressive brown eyes the ladies always loved....although, if truth be told, I've never really known what they expressed.

(HEATHER and JORDAN enter. Without the others noticing, JORDAN puts down ALTHEA's fancy blank book she had taken.)

ALTHEA: Jordan! Are you all right, dear?

HEATHER: She was breaking into the playhouse.

JORDAN: I was not!

ALTHEA: The playhouse doesn't lock.

HEATHER: Trespassing, then. Scared the crap out of me.

JORDAN: I just needed a safe place to rest.

HEATHER: Oh, girlfriend, don't we all.

ALTHEA: We have all been so worried. Your grandparents have been beside themselves.

JORDAN: I can take care of myself.

HEATHER: Ooo, you're in deep doo-doo. Grounded for life.

JORDAN: Shut up. I was looking for somebody, okay?

HEATHER: Yeah? Your soulmate? The love of your life?

JORDAN: My mother. But the address was bogus.

HEATHER: Mothers can be hard to find. Trust me.

JORDAN: Anyway, you were trespassing, too. You were going through Althea's stuff.

HEATHER *(holding up a sheaf of drawings)*: I found this in that old baby buggy. What, did you think nobody'd look?

JORDAN: I thought maybe someday Althea would find them.

(JORDAN tries to grab the drawings, but Heather won't let her. PAM enters, takes JORDAN in her arms. Pause. JORDAN tosses her headphones aside, the first time we've seen her without them, then hugs PAM again.)

PAM: We've been looking all over for you. The police are looking—

JORDAN: You called the cops on me?

PAM: We were afraid something awful had happened—

JORDAN: I'm sorry, Grandma.

(ALTHEA exits into BURT's room. We hear her singing.)

PAM: We'll talk later about how sorry you are. Right now

I'm just glad you're all right. You are all right, aren't you?

JORDAN: I guess. Am I in trouble?

PAM: Oh, yeah.

JORDAN: Is Grandpa really mad at me?

PAM: He's really scared. After you call him and tell him you're safe, he'll be really mad.

JORDAN: Me?

(PAM propels JORDAN toward the phone. JORDAN reluctantly dials. HEATHER awkwardly pats PAM's shoulder.)

HEATHER: What's Althea doing?

PAM: He must be worse.

JORDAN *(hanging up)*: No answer.

HEATHER: What'd you let it ring, once?

PAM: Call back and leave him a message.

JORDAN: Aw, Grandma—

PAM: Call back.

(JORDAN flounces to the phone, dials.)

HEATHER: It's just too weird, her singing to him like that.

JORDAN *(on the phone)*: Grandpa? Oh, I was going to leave a message. I'm here. At Althea's. I went to see my mom but there was no such address. So I just stayed in Althea's playhouse the whole time.

(ALTHEA enters, still singing softly.)

PAM: Althea? How is he?

ALTHEA: He seems peaceful.

HEATHER: Does he even know you're there?

ALTHEA: I know I'm there.

(JORDAN hangs up.)

JORDAN *(to ALTHEA)*: The whole time I was gone I kept thinking about peach ice cream.

ALTHEA: I do believe that's exactly what this complicated occasion calls for. Heather, will you help me, dear?

(HEATHER and ALTHEA exit.)

JORDAN: Grandma?

PAM: What?

JORDAN: Can I tell you something? Are you mad at me?

PAM: Yes.

JORDAN: Oh.

PAM: What did you want to tell me?

JORDAN: Nothing.

PAM: Jordan, I swear—

JORDAN: I couldn't find her, Grandma.

PAM: Your mom?

JORDAN: I went where she said she'd be, but she wasn't. There wasn't even a building there.

PAM: Oh, honey, I'm sorry.

JORDAN: I guess she got the number wrong.

PAM: I know, sweetheart. I can't find her, either.

JORDAN: Grandma?

PAM: Yes?

JORDAN: Are you going to quit teaching to write your book?

PAM: I don't know.

JORDAN: I think you should go for it.

PAM: I don't know.

JORDAN: Feed your soul, you know?

(HEATHER and ALTHEA enter with ice cream, bowls, spoons. HEATHER is talking.)

HEATHER: —okay if Tristan spends the night?

ALTHEA: Sure.

HEATHER: I told him I'd help him start a diary. He'll tell me stuff about his life and I'll write it down.

ALTHEA: That's a good idea, Heather. *(ALTHEA exits to check on BURT.)*

HEATHER: He probably won't like it.

(HEATHER and PAM dish up the ice cream. JORDAN pages through the blank book.)

JORDAN: Look.

PAM: So what did your grandpa say?

JORDAN: Nothing.

PAM: He said nothing.

HEATHER: Why do I find that hard to believe?

JORDAN: He said he's glad I'm okay and he loves me and I'm in big trouble.

HEATHER: What'd I tell you? Grounded for life.

JORDAN: Look.

(ALTHEA enters.)

ALTHEA: That's a lovely blank book. I used to have one just like it.

PAM: Jordan?

JORDAN: I found it. In the playhouse.

PAM: Jordan, that's not yours.

ALTHEA: Yes. Yes, it is.

JORDAN: Thanks, Althea.

PAM: And where are Althea's diaries?

JORDAN: In the playhouse. I brought some of them back.

HEATHER: Yeah, that was sort of bizarre.

JORDAN: I was just borrowing them. I was going to read them all the way through, just to see. Some words I can't read, though.

ALTHEA: Some words *I* can't read.

JORDAN: Some whole pages.

ALTHEA: Some whole years are more or less incomprehensible.

JORDAN: Come and look.

(PAM, HEATHER, and ALTHEA move to look at JORDAN's sketches in the blank book.)

PAM: That's you, right?

JORDAN *(paging through the book)*: So are all these, see?

HEATHER: They're all different but they all look like you. Cool.

ALTHEA: Maybe someday you could sketch my likeness. All my various likenesses.

PAM: That's a great idea, Jordan. You've always been good at art—

JORDAN: Grandma!

PAM: Sorry.

ALTHEA: I wonder if Burt would take a little ice cream. He might find it comforting. *(ALTHEA exits.)*

PAM *(to JORDAN)*: We could do a book together. I could write the text and you could illustrate it.

JORDAN: Grandma, I really suck at—

PAM: I know, honey. I'm scared, too.

HEATHER: You can't call yourself brave if you weren't scared in the first place.

PAM: Heather, that's a great line.

HEATHER: Althea told it to me.

PAM: She knows what she's talking about.

HEATHER: I want to be just like her when I grow up.

JORDAN: I don't want to be brave. Brave sucks.

HEATHER: Too bad. How about if you do my portrait sometime? Talk about scary. It'll be butt-ugly, but what the hell.

JORDAN: Okay. I guess. Okay.

PAM: Good girl.

JORDAN: Grandma!

(Offstage, ALTHEA begins the same hymn she sang when her mother was dying.)

HEATHER: He's dead. I bet you he's dead.

(JORDAN peeks into BURT's room, backs away, sits by PAM. They sit quietly while ALTHEA finishes the hymn. ALTHEA enters. JORDAN goes to her.)

ALTHEA: I said, "I love you, Burt," and I meant it, though not in the way I once did. His voice was barely audible when he said, "I love you, too." Those were his last words.

PAM: Oh, Althea.

ALTHEA: I'll need to call the boys. But not just yet. I need to sit with it a while.

PAM: If we all wrote in a journal about these last few weeks, I wonder if we'd say our lives changed, there was a "before" and an "after."

HEATHER: Nothing ever changes my life. It's always just the same old life, no matter what happens in it.

ALTHEA: Everything changes your life. *(pause.)*

JORDAN: So what do we do now?

PAM: Maybe we don't have to do anything right this minute.

(HEATHER is crying. ALTHEA puts an arm around her.)

ALTHEA: Who wants peaches on their peaches ice cream?

END OF PLAY

FRY DAY

A FULL-LENGTH PLAY IN ONE ACT

Production History

Fry Day had staged readings at the following venues:
2005, Colorado Dramatists, Denver, CO
2007, Colorado Theatre Guild New Ventures, Denver, CO
2008, Community College of Aurora, Aurora, CO
2011, The Edge Theatre: On Your Feet, Lakewood, CO
It was a finalist for the 2005 Larry Corse Playwriting Prize, Columbus State University, Columbus, OH

Characters

EMMA, the mother, late forties, early fifties, agitated, takes on the pain of those she loves.

MEREDITH, her daughter, early twenties.

MITCHELL, the father, also late forties or older.

CARNIE 1, carnival barker, runs games and souvenirs.

CARNIE 2, carnival barker, sells food.

FORTUNE TELLER, male or female, speaks in heavy fake accent.

CARNIVAL CHARACTERS, also serve, in different masks and/or costumes as CARNIVAL-GOERS and a chorus of VOICES.

SCENE ONE

DARK STAGE. Lightning strike: Flash thunderclap, burning smell. Something falls. EMMA's low cry. Lights up dim, silhouetting EMMA, who, having been struck by the lightning, is hunched over and in pain. Lights up bright on living room/dining room where EMMA was reading when the lightning struck. Her hair is wild, book on the floor, lamp tipped over. She tries to straighten, instead collapses.

EMMA: Holly, dammit, you made this so much harder!
MEREDITH *(offstage, lightly)*: Everything all right in there?
EMMA: Meredith! You're home early. What's wrong?
(EMMA struggles to get up, can't. MEREDITH enters.)
MEREDITH *(mildly concerned)*: Oh, geez, Mom. You okay?
EMMA: Just one of my spells. I'll be all right. Just let me stay here a minute. But you're home early. What's wrong?
MEREDITH: You can't stay there on the floor! How silly is that? It's embarrassing!
EMMA: You're right, honey, I'm sorry, I'll get up—
(MEREDITH helps EMMA into a chair.)
MEREDITH: Here you go. See? All better.
EMMA: Thanks, honey.
MEREDITH *(laughing)*: We used to have to step over you on our way out the door for the school bus.
EMMA: I was determined to see you girls off, no matter what. No matter what might happen during the day.
MEREDITH: We used to hate it when you did that. Especially if you thought we had a problem or something. Any little thing. Holly said not to tell you anything or we'd be tripping over you on the kitchen floor. Nobody else's mom did stuff like that. *(Beat.)*
(Bewildered.) I think I'm missing Holly—

(Lightning. EMMA winces.)

EMMA *(alarmed, cutting her off)*: Didn't you have a class? European history? Tell me about your class. What are you studying—

MEREDITH: Dropped it.

EMMA: Oh, honey, why? I thought that was your favorite class. You're doing so well. Did something happen?

MEREDITH: Not really. It's just–you know, *he's* in it. We took it together.

EMMA: The loser? The idiot? We talked about that. You're better off without him. I wish I'd known you were still sad about that.

MEREDITH: I'm not. Haven't been since I told you about it. Guy dumps you that you thought you were going to marry, you'd think you'd be sad for more than three days. I don't remember what you said, but whatever it was, it worked like magic.

EMMA: Good. I'm glad. But then why—

MEREDITH: It's just too weird seeing him every Monday, Wednesday, Friday, you know? Makes me feel kind of weird.

(Faint lightning flash. EMMA winces.)

EMMA: I can't stand it when you're sad.

MEREDITH: You can't protect me from everything, mom.

EMMA: Sure, I can. I have to. What about that Jason? You said he was interested.

MEREDITH: Omigod! Did I tell you he brought me flowers from *the grocery store*? Can you believe it?

EMMA: You're not serious.

MEREDITH: And guess where he wanted to take me for our first date? Burger King! I told him to just forget it.

EMMA: You deserve better than that.

MEREDITH *(slightly wistful)*: You know, for a fleeting moment there I thought maybe he might—

(Faint lightning. EMMA indicates pain in her head.)

(Cheery.) Oh, well, easy come easy go. Dad not home from work yet?

EMMA: Maybe he hit traffic.

MEREDITH: Maybe he's working late. Again.

EMMA: He didn't call to say so. I don't think he'd work late tonight.

MEREDITH: Whatever.

EMMA: We better get dinner on the table.

MEREDITH: You know, it won't hurt him to have to wait a few minutes.

EMMA: It comforts him to have dinner on the table when he gets home.

MEREDITH: Oh, please.

(EMMA gets up, staggers.)

(Only slightly alarmed) Now what?

EMMA: I've got one of my headaches. It's been—a rough day.

MEREDITH *(more annoyed than concerned)*: I just wish you'd go to a doctor. This is getting old.

EMMA: They don't find anything physical. It's probably just stress. *(With difficulty she makes her way toward the offstage kitchen.)*

MEREDITH: Hey, if anybody has stress headaches it ought to be me. I mean with school and the loser and Jason and everything, I'm surprised I'm not totally stressed out. But you know what? I'm not. I guess I just know how to handle stress. Cool, huh?

(EMMA steadies herself on the furniture.)

EMMA: That's good, honey. I'm glad you're feeling good. Would you mind making the salad? I'll set the table. Teamwork.

MEREDITH: I guess.

(MEREDITH exits. EMMA sets four places at the table, moving with obvious discomfort. She speaks quietly, to the absent Holly.)

EMMA: At our first house we had a big formal dining room. Do you remember that? I hadn't thought about that in—I'm not sure I really remember it anymore. I remember things *about* it— eight matching chairs; the leaf table extended to twelve feet— but I've lost the—the reality of it, how that room opened into the other rooms, how sunlight came in from the back yard through those tall windows. I think you could see it. Could you see the back yard from those windows? I can't remember. I've—oh, I've lost it.

(EMMA covers her face with her hands for a beat or two,

then shakily resumes setting the last place and exits to the kitchen. MITCHELL enters, notes the four places, circles the table touching each one. EMMA enters with food.)

Hi, honey.

(EMMA hugs him. MITCHELL doesn't pull away, but he responds only perfunctorily.)

MITCHELL: Hi.

EMMA: How was your day?

MITCHELL: Ordinary. Just a day.

EMMA: Good. That's good.

MITCHELL: Didn't really expect that. Sort of anticlimactic, actually. *(MITCHELL laughs bitterly.)*

EMMA: You almost sound disappointed, Mitchell.

MITCHELL: Just noticing my own reaction. Lack of reaction. You'd think, on this day of all days, I'd finally feel something. But then, after the first few days, I never have—

EMMA: I know—it took me a little while—I'm so sorry.

MITCHELL: Why do you keep setting four places at the table?

EMMA *(removing the place setting)*: I didn't realize—I guess it's habit. Bad habit. Oh, did that remind you—

MITCHELL *(tiredly)*: For God's sake, Emma, she's been dead—

(Lightning. EMMA cries out, drops something.)

—a long time!

EMMA: Eight years and twenty-eight days.

(She hugs him hard. After a beat, he responds mildly.)

MITCHELL: How are you doing?

EMMA: I expected it to be a hard day. As long as you and Meredith aren't suffering. She dropped her history class and that worries me, but she seems all right. Don't you think?

MITCHELL: I have no idea what's going on with Meredith.

EMMA: She's happy. I think she's happy.

MITCHELL: We used to have a lot in common, didn't we? Do I remember that right? Baseball and jazz guitar and we hiked the Grand Canyon together.

EMMA: I always wanted the four of us to be close. Holly was so independent. And look what happened.

MITCHELL *(starting to show emotion)*: It got her killed.
(Faint lightning.)
EMMA: Mitchell, don't.
MITCHELL: I'm okay. It's like being wrapped in bubble wrap and packing peanuts.
EMMA: That sounds nice.
MITCHELL: I thought today would be different. I mean, when your daughter's killer—
(EMMA kisses him to stop him from finishing the sentence.)
EMMA: Dinner's ready. Let's eat.
(MITCHELL sits. MEREDITH enters with the salad.)
MEREDITH: Hi, Daddy! *(MEREDITH hugs him from behind, playful like a small child. Same lack of response.)*
MITCHELL: Hi.
MEREDITH: Well, gee, I'm glad to see you, too.
(EMMA and MEREDITH sit.)
EMMA: I called Sears for the stove. They'll be here between noon and five Thursday. *(Beat.)* Mitchell? Did you hear me that they'll be here Thursday to fix—
MITCHELL: —the stove. Yes. Good.
EMMA: It'll be a relief to have that right front burner again. *(Beat.)* Have some of Meredith's nice salad?
MITCHELL: No, thanks.
MEREDITH *(teasing, but with an edge)*: Oh, come on, you'll hurt my feelings.
EMMA: Mitchell, you hardly eat anything. You're going to make yourself sick.
MITCHELL: I'm not hungry.
EMMA: You have to eat.
MITCHELL: Really, I'm not hungry.
MEREDITH: So how come you're not there? *(beat.)* You know, at the execution thing. They let people watch. I thought you'd want to be there.
MITCHELL: I applied. They turned me down.
EMMA: You have to apply?
MITCHELL: Some girl about Holly's age hardly gave me the time of day. Only official witnesses, she informed me.
MEREDITH: Being family doesn't make you official?

MITCHELL: You have to be approved, and there are only so many slots.

MEREDITH (*giggles*): That is so weird.

(*MITCHELL rises.*)

MITCHELL: I'm going out.

EMMA: I could make you something else. Spaghetti? You like spaghetti.

MITCHELL: Emma. I am not hungry.

MEREDITH (*sarcastic*): He is not hungry, mom.

EMMA: You have to eat. My mother got to the point where she wouldn't eat, and—

MEREDITH: He hasn't been hungry since Holly died.

MITCHELL: And all you do is eat.

MEREDITH: You don't sleep, either. I hear you at night.

MITCHELL: How would you know? You sleep twelve hours a day.

EMMA: Stop it, you two!

MITCHELL: I'll grab something to eat while I'm out.

EMMA: Where are you going?

MITCHELL: I can't stay here.

MEREDITH: Gee, Dad, thanks.

EMMA: We need to be together tonight. You aren't going to that disgusting celebration—

MITCHELL: Maybe those people know something I don't know.

MEREDITH: What people? What celebration?

MITCHELL: You can come with me if you want.

EMMA: No! Mitchell!

MEREDITH: Will somebody please tell me what's going on?

MITCHELL: Brian Mahoney is going to the electric chair tomorrow morning.

MEREDITH: I know that.

MITCHELL: All over the country tonight there are celebrations. Parties, carnivals, dancing in the streets. Countdowns.

EMMA: It's bad enough that you put yourself through that. I won't let you put Meredith in danger!

MEREDITH: Who's going to be there? Anybody I know? Anybody I'd like to know?

MITCHELL: Families and friends of his other victims, wherever they live, I guess.

MEREDITH: How many are there?

MITCHELL: I don't know. I stopped counting.

EMMA: Eight. That they know of.

MEREDITH: Counting Holly?

EMMA: Stay home, both of you. You don't know what kind of people might be there. Pickpockets, muggers—

MEREDITH: I bought some cute new clothes today I was going to show Mom.

MITCHELL: Suit yourself.

MEREDITH: And there's this brand-new shade of lipstick that just came out, and a whole new concept in skin emollient. Mom and I could have a girls' night in. What do you think, Mom?

EMMA: Ho, honey, maybe not tonight—I'm a little—tired.

MEREDITH: Come on, Mom, live a little. It'll be fun.

(MITCHELL exits. EMMA starts to follow him, stops.)

EMMA: Mitchell, don't! You'll get hurt!

MEREDITH: Jeez, talk about stuck.

EMMA: I don't know what else to do for him. Especially today.

MEREDITH: Since when is it up to you?

EMMA: It's my job. It's always been my job. And I'm pretty good at it.

MEREDITH: Most of the time I'm pretty happy, you know? Even right after she died, a few days or so, I was okay.

EMMA: I'm sorry I couldn't help you those first few days. I needed some time—

MEREDITH: But then I just sort of got on with my life. It's weird. It's like she never died. Or never lived.

EMMA: You're supposed to go on with your life.

MEREDITH: And you're not? What about your life?

EMMA: This is my life. This is what I do.

MEREDITH: So, what's up with Dad?

EMMA: If I can just get him through tonight—

MEREDITH: Until they execute the guy.

(Starts to get upset) The guy that killed my sister and—

(Lightning. EMMA doubles over. Lights down.)

SCENE TWO

Later the same evening. At rise, EMMA is sitting in the living room, looking in a mirror and putting on make-up shakily so that it gives her face a slightly distorted, clownish appearance. MEREDITH is offstage, talking.

MEREDITH: —looked so cute in the store but you can't tell till you get stuff home. They have trick mirrors that make you look better so you'll buy. But half the fun is taking things back and shopping all over again. I just can't decide about these pants— *(MEREDITH enters, modeling.)* What do you think about these pants? Are they too tight?

EMMA: Turn around, let me see. No, they look good on you.

MEREDITH: Your lipstick is smeared.

EMMA: Is it? Oh, dear.

MEREDITH: Got a hot date?

EMMA: I might join your father. I thought I'd just put my face on.

MEREDITH: You said you'd look at my new clothes.

EMMA: Later, after we're finished.

MEREDITH: You're going to this carnival thing?

EMMA: They're calling it an execution party.

MEREDITH: You are not serious. *(Beat.)* Well, is this invitation only or can I go?

EMMA: It's not a safe place for you to be. And I don't think it will be much fun.

MEREDITH: Are you sure these pants don't make me look fat?

EMMA: Everything looks good on you, honey. I wish I had your figure.

MEREDITH: I don't have the right underwear, though. Is there a panty line?

EMMA: I don't see—well, maybe a little.

MEREDITH *(exits)*: The right underwear is so important, you know? It can make or break an entire outfit. Want to go with me to Victoria's Secret tomorrow?

EMMA: I appreciate the invitation, I really do, but I don't think I'll be up to that.

MEREDITH: Oh, Mom, come on! You can help me pick out some sexy thongs and camisoles and bras. It'll be fun! I thought you'd always be there for me.

EMMA: Tomorrow's not a good day.

MEREDITH: What's going on tomorrow?

EMMA: It's just that I won't be getting much sleep tonight.

MEREDITH: Too much partying, hmmm?

EMMA: Just—keeping watch, I guess.

MEREDITH: You know, he's gonna fry whether you're awake or not. You might as well get your beauty rest. Hasn't he already stolen enough?

(Faint lightning. EMMA winces, smearing make-up. MEREDITH enters in a new outfit.)

(Starting to be sad and scared.) Mom? Mom? I just now remembered that time Holly took me clothes shopping for my thirteenth birthday. We were gone all day, and we went to a zillion stores, and we had lunch at Hard Rock. It was so fun.

(She is becoming agitated. Lightning flashes all around. EMMA is in pain.)

I forgot all about that! How could I forget? Now I see she had sort of funky taste in clothes, but back then I thought she knew everything about everything. My next birthday I had to go shopping all by myself.

EMMA: I offered to go with you, but you didn't want me to.

MEREDITH: Oh, God, I miss her!

(Lightning strike. EMMA cries out and drops the mirror.)

(Beat. Cheery again.) Wow, that was kind of weird. Like that memory just struck me and then went away. You okay, Mom?

EMMA: I need—to lie down.

MEREDITH *(modeling)*: Wait, does this outfit work?

(EMMA sinks to the floor.)

Oh, please, not that falling-on-the-floor routine. You can't see anything from there.

EMMA: It looks fine, dear.

MEREDITH: Don't give me "fine"! "Fine" doesn't tell me anything! *(MEREDITH helps EMMA back into the chair.)*

EMMA: The colors are good on you.

MEREDITH: Do you really think so?

EMMA: With your coloring, the shade your hair is now. It's nice.

MEREDITH: Your face is totally messed up. Wait right here and I'll go get that new skin care system I bought today, and we'll start over.

EMMA: I need to rest, conserve my strength—

MEREDITH (*exits*): I'll be right back!

(*Unsteadily EMMA retrieves the mirror, looks at herself, wipes vaguely at her face. MEREDITH enters carrying a large fancy make-up case, arrays various products and equipment on the table, begins cleaning EMMA's face.*)

I got manicure and pedicure stuff, too. We can paint our toenails! This'll be fun!

SCENE THREE

Jaunty music up first, then bright lights. Carnival midway, somewhat surrealistic. Concessions, game booths, carousel, etc. May be suggested rather than built.

Mitchell enters, wearing a completely blank, featureless, neutral-color mask. His clothes are also neutral in color and cover all his skin.

CARNIE 1: Brian Mahoney's dancing bears right here right there! Flip the switch and watch him twitch!

(*MITCHELL joins the crowd at the booth.*)

MITCHELL: My daughter loves carnivals.

CARNIE 1: What's the game? What's her name?

MITCHELL: Holly.

CARNIE 1: Dolly, Molly, Polly, Lolly.

MITCHELL: It's Holly. With an h.

CARNIE 1: Three chances to win. You out or you in?

(*MITCHELL gives him money in exchange for three multicolored balls, then stands there, tossing the balls from one hand to the other with increasing force. CARNIE 1 resumes his pitch to other potential customers.*)

MITCHELL: What's the trick?

CARNIE 1: No trick, no scam, no shill. This here's a game of skill.

MITCHELL: Bullshit. Do I look like an idiot? It's rigged. Everything's rigged.

CARNIE 1: You ain't gonna play, get outta the way.

(CARNIE 1 goes back to working the crowd. MITCHELL throws the three balls as hard as he can and waits for a moment.)

MITCHELL: Nothing. *(He walks away.)*

CARNIE 1: Sorry, pal, that's lady luck. Next player! Step right up!

(MITCHELL continues along the midway, encountering various oddities—perhaps strange balloon animals and people, clowns with slightly grotesque features, sword- and fire-swallowers, someone juggling balls painted with happy and sad faces. These characters come from all over the theater, including from the audience. MITCHELL copies each briefly.)

FORTUNE TELLER *(in a heavy, fake accent)*: Sonny, sonny, over here! Come and look into your future!

MITCHELL: I can already see into my future. Thanks anyway.

FORTUNE TELLER: No no no no no, come back here! I tell your fortune for five small dollahs!

MITCHELL: Okay, sure. What have I got to lose, other than five small dollahs? *(MITCHELL pays and sits at the booth.)*

FORTUNE TELLER: Give me your hand.

(Pause. Carnival characters pass by.)

MITCHELL: Don't tell me. You see a short, pale stranger named Brian Joseph Mahoney.

FORTUNE TELLER: Your lifeline, it is long and strong.

MITCHELL *(sarcastically)*: Great.

FORTUNE TELLER: You will have a long and happy life. There you go.

(She tries to drop his hand, but he won't let her.)

MITCHELL: So, can you see the past as well as the future?

FORTUNE TELLER: Yes, yes, something terrible happened to you. I sense that you are very sad. That's all now.

MITCHELL: Not even close.

FORTUNE TELLER: Very very sad, yes, but you will see her

again on the other side, she waits for you in a gown of light—

MITCHELL: If I'd come to you eight years and twenty-nine days ago, could you have foretold what happened to my daughter?

FORTUNE TELLER (*coyly*): Maybe, maybe not. Nevah can tell.

MITCHELL: All of it? Everything that happened to her before we even knew she was missing?

FORTUNE TELLER: I see many things, mistah.

MITCHELL: And could you have foretold that after the first couple of days I wouldn't feel anything? I don't feel anything. Why am I telling this to a carnival gypsy?

FORTUNE TELLER: We hold hands, I tell you things, you tell me things. That's how it works. Five small dollahs. Such a deal.

MITCHELL: Did you know the word "gyp" is a racist term? Because it comes from "gypsy"? (*MITCHELL starts to get up.*)

FORTUNE TELLER: Tell you what, sonny. Five more small dollahs, I read the cards for you.

MITCHELL: I should be home with my wife and daughter.

FORTUNE TELLER: Your daughter is dead.

MITCHELL: My other daughter.

FORTUNE TELLER: Ah, your other daughter, what will happen to her? What will you feel about what will happen to her? Five more small dollahs, I look and see. No gyp. Such a deal.

MITCHELL: She was dead before I even knew she was missing. It got past me.

FORTUNE TELLER (*drops the accent*): Why are you telling me this, man?

MITCHELL: Will your cards say when Brian Joseph Mahoney's going to die? The exact moment, so I don't miss that, too? That'd be worth five small dollahs.

FORTUNE TELLER: Shit, I got no time for this. I got a business to run here, know what I'm sayin'? We're real busy tonight.

MITCHELL: So, you can't tell me that?

FORTUNE TELLER: Five o'clock in the a.m. is what I heard on the news.

MITCHELL: That's when they're scheduled to throw the switch. But will there be delays? Mechanical problems? Stays? And how long will it take him to die? When, precisely, will his spirit leave his body?

FORTUNE TELLER: Hell if I know.

(MITCHELL kisses the FORTUNE TELLER's hand and leaves the booth.)

(Accent again, to one of the CARNIVAL CHARACTERS): Hey, there, little lady, step right up and see your future! Five small dollahs!

(MITCHELL goes on along the midway, stops as a spot comes up on a food booth with a huge sign saying "Fryin' Brians $2.00.")

MITCHELL: *What* are fryin' Brians?

CARNIE 2: Corn dogs. Kind of look like Brian Mahoney's dick, don't you think?

MITCHELL: I've never seen his dick. Holly did, though.

CARNIE 2: Two bucks apiece, dude. What's your pleasure?

MITCHELL *(hesitates)*: Not hungry. *(MITCHELL starts to turn away.)*

CARNIE 2: So didja hear the one about Brian Mahoney?

MITCHELL: I've heard a lot about Brian Mahoney.

CARNIE 2: Didja hear he didn't know what day it was?

MITCHELL: What?

CARNIE 2: Come on, man, this is a good one. Ask me why he didn't know what day it was.

MITCHELL: Okay. Why didn't Brian Mahoney know what day it was?

CARNIE 2: Because he thought it was fry day!

(Jeers and hoots of laughter. After a moment, MITCHELL joins in. Carousel lights swirl throughout the audience.)

CARNIE 1: Mahoney masks! Get 'em while they last!

(Masks made out of brown paper bags, hideous to the point of being ludicrous, are tossed around the stage. MITCHELL picks up one after another and puts them on over his own mask.)

Mahoney dolly for little Molly?

(A long string of gigantic paper dolls without features is pulled from one side of the stage to the other. MITCHELL breaks the string, grabs a paper hand in each of his, and becomes part of the string for a

few moments, bobbing and dancing, until he drops the hands and the dolls fall.)

Straps for the hands, straps for the feet, just like the real thing, buy the kids a treat!

FORTUNE TELLER (*from the back of the audience, with accent)*: Sonny, sonny, hey, sonny, the cards show something very important happen to you! Verrrry im-por-tant! Don't miss it now!

CARNIE 2: Last chance to play, dude! Time's runnin' out!

FORTUNE TELLER: Polly!

CARNIE 1: Dolly!

CARNIE 2: Lolly!

FORTUNE TELLER: Molly!

(Whoops and shouts of "Fry Day! Fry Day!" From CARNIE 1, CARNIE 2, FORTUNE TELLER, and CARNIVAL CHARACTERS onstage and throughout the audience. MITCHELL hesitantly joins in. Gradually everyone else subsides and drifts offstage, leaving MITCHELL chanting alone. Lights down slowly. Then MITCHELL's chanting fades.)

SCENE FOUR

Later the same evening. Meredith and EMMA in the living room. At rise MEREDITH is talking while she paints her toenails.

MEREDITH: —lace on the sleeves and pearl buttons from neckline to hemline. Ooh, it's so pretty!

EMMA: It does sound lovely.

MEREDITH: But I just can't decide about the color, you know? It's this kind of pinkish-gray, or grayish-pink, mauve, I guess, or taupe, and I just don't know if it works for me. Maybe I should get my colors done. *(Beat.)* What do you think?

EMMA: Think about what?

MEREDITH: What I just said? Whether I should get my colors done? So, I know whether to buy this dress or not?

EMMA: Colors. Oh. Well, I don't know—if you want to have your colors done, of course you should. I guess.

MEREDITH: Mom, this is important! You're not even listening.

EMMA: I'm listening.

MEREDITH *(sarcastically)*: I'm sorry if I'm boring you. I know you've got more important things on your mind than me tonight.

EMMA: Nonsense, Meredith, you are what keeps me going. You and your father.

MEREDITH: He hates me.

EMMA: He does not hate you. He adores you.

MEREDITH: He's always mad at me.

EMMA: That's what he says about you. What am I going to do with the two of you?

MEREDITH: Tell him to be nice to me.

EMMA: I have, just like I tell you to be nice to him. It breaks my heart. I so much want you to be close—

MEREDITH: We used to be. Didn't we?

EMMA: You used to have fun together. Skiing and swimming and hiking and silly movies. You and Holly both. A lot of times I felt left out, but that's okay. I loved watching you with your daddy.

MEREDITH: I want him to love me again!

(Faint lightning. EMMA flinches.)

EMMA: I'll talk to him again, honey! Don't be sad! I'll fix it!

MEREDITH: Okay. *(MEREDITH finishes the toenails on one foot, holds it out for EMMA's admiration.)* See?

EMMA: Nice glitter!

MEREDITH: I'll finish the other foot and then we'll do yours.

EMMA: I've never liked this sort of thing.

MEREDITH: You'll like this. Trust me.

EMMA: I don't think so, honey. I'm not feeling—

MEREDITH: You know what's sort of weird? Most of the time I don't even miss her.

EMMA: I can miss her for all of us.

MEREDITH: I mean, sometimes it seems like I'm going to miss her, and I even start to feel sad—

EMMA *(appalled)*: You do?

MEREDITH: —but it never goes very far and it's gone like that. *(MEREDITH snaps her fingers.)* It's like sadness just flies out of me, every time it gets close. Like it's pulled out of me, or deflected, or something.

EMMA *(relieved)*: Good. That's good.

MEREDITH: Is it? You and dad are really sad—

EMMA: Your father is not sad. I won't allow it. I can't stand it. He's not sad, you hear me?

MEREDITH: Okay, okay, he's not sad. He's a zombie.

EMMA: But he's not sad.

MEREDITH *(increasingly upset)*: Anyway, I see how—how you and dad are about Holly, and sometimes I think, you know, she was my sister, so how come I don't feel like that? It's like somebody stole my sister from me and then somebody stole my—my sorrow from me, too!

(Lightning. EMMA reacts.)

EMMA: Meredith—

MEREDITH: Oh, God, there it is! Holly! I miss her! I miss my big sister! Why did she have to—

(Lightning. EMMA gasps and holds her head.)

Mom? You okay?

EMMA: I need to lie down.

MEREDITH: Wait a sec, I want to show you that catalogue with the dresses.

EMMA: First thing tomorrow, honey, okay? I promise, I'll look at them tomorrow.

MEREDITH: Maybe I have plans tomorrow. I need your opinion tonight. And you promised I could do your toenails.

EMMA: My head—I can't—

MEREDITH: You know what? My life is just as important as her death. It is.

EMMA: Of course it is—

MEREDITH: Maybe I'll just go to that execution party thing.

EMMA: No, please, I want you to stay home where I can keep you safe.

MEREDITH: Sounds like fun! Roller coasters and cotton candy and those stupid games? What do you call that thing that you hit with a mallet and if it goes all the way to the top and makes the bell ring you win? That guy who took me to the carnival last summer didn't win me a single thing. I really wanted one of those cute panda bears, too. So much for him. Talk about a loser.

EMMA: People all over the country are celebrating the— about Mahoney—it's an event, like when they used to have public hangings and people would come with their children and bring picnic lunches.

MEREDITH: Holly took me to a carnival once. She won all kinds of stuff. I think she won me something, some huge ball or stuffed animal or something, bigger than I was, but I don't know whatever happened to it. Holly always won. *(MEREDITH giggles.)* Well, not always, I guess.

EMMA: Will you be all right tonight?

MEREDITH: Me? Sure. I'm always all right. I have to try my new skin care system. That'll fill the evening.

EMMA: Then I need to lie down and wait. If you're all right.

MEREDITH: Sure. Go ahead. Whatever.

(EMMA exits somewhat unsteadily.)

This is really getting old, you know that?

(Faint carnival lights and carousel music up.)

A carnival might be interesting. But I have to do my skin care.

(MEREDITH exits. Stage lights down, leaving just the suggestion of carnival lights and music. From throughout the theater we hear...)

VOICES: Fry day fry day fry day fry day

FORTUNE TELLER *(offstage)*: Your past, your present, and your future! Come and get 'em! Such a deal!

CARNIE 1 *(offstage)*: Ladies and gentlemen, come on down! We got electric chairs! We got clowns!

CARNIE 2 *(offstage)*: Step right up, dudes and dudettes! It's the Brian Mahoney show! And you're the star!

(From the audience, EMMA makes her way to the stage.)

EMMA: I shouldn't have let him go without me. But sometimes, sometimes, my grief is too good to share. I want it all. *(EMMA enters a downstage spot.)* It's enormous. It's exquisite. It fills me. I need it all.

(Lights up full on dining room. Meredith enters, face covered with facial clay, hair wrapped in a towel.)

Dammit, Holly, you could have taken the bus. Did you think I wouldn't find out? I checked, and the bus went right by there. But hitchhiking was an "adventure," wasn't it? You met "the most interesting people," didn't you?

MEREDITH *(overlapping)*: — the most interesting people.

EMMA: People with stories.

MEREDITH *(overlapping)*: People with stories. People things actually happen to.

EMMA: You used to bring those stories home, like feral kittens.

MEREDITH: There was this woman—

EMMA: I'd turn out your pockets and go through your purse and read your diary, do everything I could to get rid of all those stories before they hurt somebody.

MEREDITH: —this sculptor with—

EMMA: I'd try to scrub them out, pick them out with tweezers but

MEREDITH: Long, pure white, tangled hair.

EMMA: No matter what I did they'd still be there—

MEREDITH: The back of her pickup

EMMA: Loose threads and dry skin

MEREDITH: Was piled high with faces.

EMMA: And dust mites—

MEREDITH: Disfigured faces.

EMMA: And millions of accumulated dust motes—

MEREDITH: Misshapen faces.

EMMA: And stories—

MEREDITH: Hideous and beautiful—*(Beat.)*

EMMA: Meredith? Did Holly tell you that?

MEREDITH: Well, she could have. It's the kind of thing that could have happened to her.

EMMA: She promised me she wouldn't tell you any of her stories. Contaminate you with her wildness, that need to get away.

MEREDITH: She didn't. I don't know how anything was for her. Living or dying. All I can do is make it up, and I can only do that once in a while.

EMMA: I never heard anything about a white-haired sculptor in a pickup truck filled with—

MEREDITH: Mom, it's my story. Don't you get it? I'm making it up.

EMMA: —filled with faces.

MEREDITH *(overlapping)*: —faces.

(As MEREDITH describes each facial feature, she peels the clay from that part of her own face.)

In the cab with us were pieces of faces. Ears rolling around under our feet. Noses jumbled between us on the seat. Eyeballs dangling from the visors and mirrors and gear shift.

EMMA: Meredith? Honey? This didn't really happen to you, did it?

MEREDITH *(increasingly into it)*: Teeth bobbling on the dashboard!

EMMA: I didn't know!

MEREDITH: Glove compartment stuffed with tongues!

EMMA: I'm so sorry!

MEREDITH *(unwrapping the towel from her hair)*: Hair all over the windshield! I can't see out! Long pure white beautiful hair!

EMMA: No!

(EMMA readies herself to intercept MEREDITH's pain. Instead of lightning, carousel lights begin to swirl around the audience.)

MEREDITH (*perky*): I just made that up. Not bad, huh?
(Lights down gradually on dining room. MEREDITH and EMMA exit. Lights and music up on carnival midway.)

SCENE FIVE

Midway, characters still in masks.
MITCHELL mills among other CARNIVAL-GOERS. A chant about Brian Mahoney starts and MITCHELL joins in.

MITCHELL and CARNIVAL-GOERS: Hey hey hey, Mahoney's gonna pay! Hi hi hi, Mahoney's gonna fry!
(After a few seconds the chant falls apart, leaving MITCHELL continuing it on his own, trying to encourage others, including random audience members.)
MITCHELL: Hey, hey, whaddaya know? Brian Mahoney's gonna go! Come on, everybody, help me out here! Hey, hey, whaddaya know—
(Finally MITCHELL gives up.)
CARNIE 2: Ladies and gentlemen! History happening before your very eyes!
CARNIE 1: Flip the switch and watch him twitch!
(As MITCHELL approaches a shadowed booth, spot up on sign: "Mahoney's cajones," which can be any kind of soft candy spheres, hot, e.g. cinnamon.)
MITCHELL *(laughs)*: Mahoney's cajones?
CARNIE 2: Little balls o' fire! Get 'em while they're fresh!
MITCHELL: Give me all you've got.
CARNIE 2: You wanna be careful there, buddy. These is strong little buggers. Burn yer belly right through.
MITCHELL: Trust me, I've had worse. I won't even feel it.
CARNIE 2: Tough guy, huh? Okay, you got it. Sold. Don't say I didn't warn ya.
(CARNIE 2 hands MITCHELL a large sack and fills it with the rest of the candy.)
Here ya go. Every last one.
(CARNIE 2 shows MITCHELL and the audience that the container is empty and takes down the "Mahoney's cajones" sign.)
MITCHELL: Keep the change.
CARNIE 2: Ha. No change comin', buddy. I give 'em to ya at cost, yer such a tough guy.

MITCHELL: Yeah? Well, thanks.

(CARNIE 2 waves him away. As soon as MITCHELL has moved on, CARNIE 2 brings out another big container of "Mahoney's cajones" and puts the sign back up.)

CARNIE 2: Suck-er.

MITCHELL: Hot, he said. Ha. This is nothing. What a gyp.

(MITCHELL eats the candy, grimacing at how hot it really is. Sound of someone hitting a platform with a mallet, followed by a loud gong. The crowd cheers.)

CARNIE 2: Ladies and gentlemen! It's midnight! The countdown begins!

(Sound of a clock striking midnight, bridging into the next scene.)

CARNIE 1: The hour has struck and we're in luck!

(Clapping and chanting ("Ho ho, hey, hey, Brian Mahoney dies today") erupt throughout the theater. Mitchell begins throwing "Mahoney's cajones" into the audience. Lights down.)

SCENE SIX

As the clock finishes striking midnight, lights up dim on the living room where EMMA has fallen asleep on the couch. Throughout this scene, faint lightning all around. MEREDITH enters, dressed to go out with open-toed shoes to show off her toenails, trying to fasten a pendant around her neck.

MEREDITH: Hey, Mom, can you fasten this for me? It's got this weird clasp. *(EMMA doesn't wake up.)* Mom! I need you here!

EMMA *(stirring)*: You look nice, dear.

MEREDITH: You always say that. You're not even looking. *(EMMA sits up with difficulty.)*

EMMA: You look really pretty. I like that shirt on you.

MEREDITH: Will you fasten this for me, please?

EMMA *(fastening the clasp)*: This is Holly's.

MEREDITH: Not any more.

EMMA: She brought it home from Alaska. There was some sort of story attached to it, but I was just so relieved she was home safe. I wish I'd paid more attention.

MEREDITH: Something about how a bear tore the world open and human life was created. Or maybe it was a crow. Oh, remember Holly's pet crow? What was his name?

EMMA: She said it wasn't a pet, she didn't own it, didn't have naming rights. You called it Jesse Jim, when she was out of earshot.

MEREDITH: Did I?

EMMA: Because it stole things. Anything shiny. Once it was your brand-new watch. We never did find it.

MEREDITH: And your car keys. One time I was supposed to meet some guy, and he ended up having to come and get me because Jesse Jim took your car keys. Holly found them, like two weeks later.

EMMA: Are you okay, remembering that? *(Lightning is getting brighter.)*

MEREDITH *(beginning to show distress)*: Holly said I had to accept that it was just his nature. She thought it was cute. Even when he stole her contact case—remember that? She never did find it.

EMMA: Your sister has always demanded a lot from everyone.

MEREDITH: "You have to go into things, not away from them. You have to live life all the way." You know what? I don't have to do shit!

EMMA: Holly never does anything halfway.

MEREDITH: She was an intensity junkie. If there wasn't some big thing going on, she'd make something happen, so she could "live it all the way" and tell everybody else how to live it, too. It got really old.

EMMA: She stretches us.

MEREDITH (*increasingly angry*): Pushed people around, is more like it. Took over our lives. And she's still getting away with it. She'd love all this drama all about her.

EMMA: She didn't do it on purpose.

MEREDITH: You and Dad always did like her best.

EMMA: That's not true! It's just that you've always been easier. Holly takes more energy.

MEREDITH: She took more of everything. Attention. Air. Space in the world. Maybe I should thank what's-his-face.

EMMA: My God, Meredith! How can you say such a thing?

MEREDITH: But now that she's gone I don't know what to do. My life doesn't make any sense without her—

(*Lightning flash. EMMA gasps. Beat.*)

EMMA (*weakly, trying to redirect MEREDITH*): Are you going out? It's awfully late.

MEREDITH (*perky, no longer upset*): I'm going to the carnival.

EMMA: Oh, Meredith, no!

MEREDITH (*giggles*): Excuse me, I mean the execution party.

EMMA: It's dangerous for you there.

MEREDITH: Dad's there.

EMMA: It's dangerous for him, too. Who knows what can happen in a place like that on a night like this?

MEREDITH: Oh, please. What could happen? You're such a worry wart. It's just a carnival. Maybe Dad will win me something.

EMMA (*desperately*): Come here and let me fix your hair.

MEREDITH: What's wrong with my hair?

EMMA: It just looks a little—funky. Not very flattering.

MEREDITH (*peering into a mirror from her purse*): Oh, no, does it?! I am having sort of a bad hair day, it's a little staticky, but I used finishing spray—

EMMA: You don't look your best.

MEREDITH: I can't go out like this!

EMMA: Bring me a brush and some clips and I'll see what I can do.

MEREDITH (*exiting*): I don't want to be late!

EMMA: It's supposed to go on all night, until he's—until it's over.

MEREDITH (*offstage*): I don't want to miss anything!

EMMA (*quietly*): Maybe you'll miss it all.

(*MEREDITH enters with much hair equipment and sits on the floor at EMMA's feet.*)

MEREDITH: Remember my first date?

EMMA: You went to a movie with that sweet Matthews boy.

MEREDITH: Ryan Matthews wasn't all that sweet. He was pretty much all about himself. But that wasn't my first date. I can't believe you don't remember, Mom. My first date was the Valentine's Dance in sixth grade.

EMMA: That wasn't a date. You went with a group of girls.

MEREDITH: I met Tyler Bernstein there. It was a date.

EMMA: I wasn't aware of that.

MEREDITH: Well, Holly was aware of that. She insisted on fixing my hair. Tyler was waiting for me at school, and he kept calling and I kept saying I'd be there in a few, but she did all these weird things to my hair, feathers and beads and combs and crimps and curls in bizarre places.

EMMA: Combs can be nice.

MEREDITH: For Holly, maybe, she had all that hair. I hated everything she did to my head. She'd put stuff in and I'd pull it out, and she'd do things with the curling iron and the crimping iron and I'd go stick my head under the faucet and then she'd blow-dry it again and it would be all wild, and we were yelling at each other and Tyler kept calling and I thought I was going to have a nervous breakdown.

EMMA: Where was I?

MEREDITH: You were gone somewhere. You left me with her.

EMMA: Your hair really is full of static tonight. I think you're going to have to wash it and use some of that leave-in conditioner.

MEREDITH: I don't have time!

EMMA: Maybe we can spray it. *(EMMA sprays MEREDITH's hair.)*

MEREDITH: She finally did a French braid and it looked really good. I was like two hours late getting to the dance, but Tyler was still waiting for me and he said I looked great.

EMMA: I really don't remember Tyler Bernstein at all.

MEREDITH: That was our first and last date. He never called again.

EMMA: Oh, honey, I'm sorry! Did that hurt your feelings?

MEREDITH: I got over it. God, Mom, I'm dripping!

EMMA: Did I use too much? I was trying to get it to stay in place. If you want to wash and dry it, I can try again.

MEREDITH: I don't have time for that! People aren't going to wait for me like Tyler did. I'm just going to have to go looking like shit. Thanks a lot, Mom. I hope you're happy. *(MEREDITH exits. EMMA starts after her.)*

EMMA: Please, Meredith, don't go! Stay home with me where I can— *(EMMA stops.)*

Tyler Bernstein. What else have I missed, Holly? If I'd known what was happening to you maybe I could have taken away the pain and the fear, at least, even if I couldn't stop it. But I missed it. I didn't know until it was too late.

(Lightning and thunderclap. Lights down except for spot on EMMA as she cries out and collapses. During the following monologue she reveals a fresh burn from the pain she has absorbed in the form of lightning. CARNIES speak from darkness.)

Once upon a time there was a little girl named Emma who lived with her mommy in a great big house. Just the two of them in that great big house, and the little girl loved her mommy more than anything in the whole world, and her mommy was very sad, very sad, very sad. In that house there were many many rooms with wonderful names, parlor and pantry and library and sun room and moon room and mud room and water room and dark room and light room and junk room and treasure room and play room and music room and porch. And in every room the little girl always found her mommy, and her mommy was always sad.

CARNIE 1: Sad is bad.

EMMA: The mommy got sad about a lot of things. A certain kind of light that the little girl didn't see could make her cry and cry. One time she got so sad about the taste of strawberries that she didn't get out of bed for four whole days. The mommy would get really scared, too. Scared of the letter z. Scared of elephants. Scared of what had happened to her before the little girl was born and what was happening now and what was going to happen. It was the little girl's job to make the mommy happy and to make the mommy feel safe. Sometimes the little girl didn't know how to do that, and then the mommy got mad. Not mean mad or loud mad or hurting mad, but kind of sad mad. So it was the little girl's job to keep her mommy from being mad, too.

CARNIE 2: Mad is bad.

CARNIE 1 (*from darkness*): Sad mad is bad.

CARNIE 1 and CARNIE 2: Mad sad is bad.

EMMA: Then one day there was a great big storm, and it rained really hard, and there was thunder and lightning and trees fell down and the roof leaked and the mommy was sad and scared and mad, and the little girl didn't know what to do, didn't know what to do, didn't know what to do! And then all of a sudden—

(*Lightning strike. EMMA cries out, shows an old scar at her navel, the first scar.*)

—I found out I could make it come to me instead! I could make the sad and the scared and the mad come to me instead of to Mommy, and then Mommy was happy! I could make Mommy happy! I was magic! The little girl was magic!

(*Lightning all around. EMMA shrieks with joy and raises her arms. Spot down on EMMA. Sound of a gong striking one as lights come up on CARNIE 1, CARNIE 2, FORTUNE TELLER, MEREDITH, and MITCHELL at the carnival.*)

MEREDITH: What's that?

CARNIE 2: Countdown!

CARNIE 1: One o'clock and all is well. Mahoney's on his way to Hell.

VOICES (*whispering from throughout the theater*): Fry day fry day fry day fry day

MITCHELL (*to MEREDITH*): What are you doing here? I thought you had important things to do.

(*MITCHELL takes MEREDITH's hand to inspect her nails, drops it. She holds out a foot to show her toenails, teeters, grabs MITCHELL for balance and they both stagger. MEREDITH shrieks playfully. MITCHELL turns away.*)

MEREDITH: What are *you* doing here?

MITCHELL: I don't know.

FORTUNE TELLER (*with heavy fake accent*): Right over here, right over here! For just five dollahs and five minutes of your time, I see into your future!

MEREDITH: Mom says it's dangerous here.

MITCHELL: She's probably right.

MEREDITH: Yeah, but mom thinks everything's dangerous.

MITCHELL: She's probably right.

(*Throughout the following exchange, various CARNIVAL CHARACTERS enter and exit, cheesy and not very good at what they do: Maybe a juggler who eventually drops everything, a snake handler with obviously fake snakes, a contortionist who gets stuck in a box, etc.*)

MEREDITH: She's just always *there*. Even when I'm away from her I can feel her. God!

MITCHELL: She wants to shield you from pain. Parents do that.

MEREDITH: She does it to you, too. She can't stand it when you're even a little bit down. Like we're out of half-and-half for your coffee.

CARNIE 1: Sad is bad.

MITCHELL: That's how your mother loves. There are worse ways.

MEREDITH: She gets on my last nerve.

MITCHELL: Don't diss your mother.

MEREDITH: Diss, dad? What are you some kind of a rapper? Diss?

MITCHELL: You'd fall apart if it wasn't for her. You couldn't stand it.

MEREDITH: Stand what? What are you talking about?

MITCHELL: Life.

CARNIE 1 *(with a rap beat)*: Bad hair days and loser boyfriends/boring English class and poison.

CARNIE 2: Holly Holly Holly Holly

MITCHELL: You have no idea what real life is.

MEREDITH: Oh, and you do? Daddy zombie?

MITCHELL: I was seriously depressed when I met your mother.

MEREDITH: How depressed?

MITCHELL: Suicidal.

MEREDITH: Oh, please. Everybody I know says that at one time or another.

MITCHELL: I have the scars to prove it.

MEREDITH: Yeah? Show me.

MITCHELL: I don't think so.

MEREDITH: Why not?

MITCHELL: I don't like to think about it. Besides, it's private.

MEREDITH: You've got scars on your private parts? You tried to kill yourself through your crotch? Oooh, daddy!

MITCHELL: Through my heart. Near my heart—I missed. And through the roof of my mouth.

MEREDITH *(impressed)*: Wow.

MITCHELL: It's not something I'm proud of.

MEREDITH: Mom's scars are pretty disgusting. She needs a few nips and tucks if you ask me.

MITCHELL: They're just part of who she is.

MEREDITH: Where'd she get them? Maybe I don't want to know.

MITCHELL: I don't know. She doesn't talk about it.

MEREDITH: You've been married for like a hundred years and you don't know? Gee, the two of you must be really close.

MITCHELL: I think something happened with her mother when she was growing up, but I'm just guessing.

(EMMA enters. They don't see her.)

MEREDITH: That martyr thing she does gets old.

MITCHELL: She saved my life.

MEREDITH: What'd she do, grab the gun?

MITCHELL: She put herself between me and the pain, somehow. Absorbed it, or deflected it, or something. I don't know how she does it, but she's good at it. She told me—

EMMA: —you've been hurt enough for one lifetime.

MITCHELL: She told me—

EMMA: —I can make it all better.

MITCHELL: She told me—

EMMA: —you won't ever have to hurt again.

MITCHELL: It was love at first sight.

MITCHELL and EMMA: For both of us.

MEREDITH: Ooh, that's so romantic! It's weird to think of my parents in love like that!

MITCHELL *(beginning to show emotion)*: Then Holly died.

(EMMA pantomimes deflecting his pain to herself. MITCHELLL subsides.)

MEREDITH: So, what exactly happened to her, anyway?

MITCHELL: What are you talking about? You know what happened.

MEREDITH: I know he killed her. That Brian Mahoney dude. And raped her—

EMMA: Don't talk about it! Don't think about it!

MEREDITH: But nobody ever told me the whole story.

EMMA: You don't need to know that. It will just hurt you.

MEREDITH: She was my sister.

(A sword-swallower enters, hands the sword to MEREDITH who begins to insert it into her mouth. MITCHELL takes the sword and makes cutting motions down his arms and legs. Red appears, suggesting blood. EMMA throws the sword offstage.)

(Lights down. Gong strikes two.)

VOICES *(from throughout the theater)*: Two!

CARNIE 2: Ladies! And! Gentlemen! We are pleased and proud to unveil our newest attraction!

CARNIE 1: One of a kind! Custom designed!

CARNIE 2: A game of skill and endurance.

CARNIE 1: Chutzpah and moxie! Don't play it by proxy!

FORTUNE TELLER: Such a deal!

CARNIE 2: Call it imaginative courage.

CARNIE 1: Test the best and screw the rest.

CARNIE 2: Listen up now. Here's the rules.

CARNIE 1: Rules for the fools. Fools for the rules.

CARNIE 2: When you—

CARNIE 1 *(interrupting)*: In finishing schools!

CARNIE 2: When you hear—

CARNIE 1 *(vastly pleased to be thinking of more rhymes)*: Goblins and ghouls! Belts full of tools! Reflected in pools!

CARNIE 2 *(shouts over CARNIE 1)*: When you hear this sound—

(Sound of triangle ding.)

CARNIE 1: Family jewels!

CARNIE 2: —whenever you hear that sound, you have five seconds to tell a story of how Holly died.

CARNIE 1: Dolly Wally Jolly Tolly Molly

EMMA: No!

MITCHELL: It's Holly. With an h.

(MEREDITH and MITCHELL move downstage together to listen. Triangle dings.)

CARNIE 2: Five seconds! Who's first?

CARNIE 1: Hey, hey, whaddaya know? Ready, steady, set, and go!

(The following guesses come from throughout the theater. Each is preceded by the ding of the triangle.)

VOICE: Car accident!

CARNIE 2: Wrrrrong!

VOICE: Heart attack!

CARNIE 1: Nope! Dope!

VOICE: Plane crash!

FORTUNE TELLER: Sorry, no!

VOICE: Suicide!

CARNIE 2: Incorrect!

VOICES: Flesh-eating disease! House fire! Getting shot out of a cannon!

CARNIE 1 *(makes the sound of a buzzer indicating a wrong*

answer): Maaa! Maaa! Maaa! Maaa!

MEREDITH *(with some emotion)*: She was hitchhiking and Brian Joseph Mahoney gave her a ride. Is that right?

(Lightning.)

EMMA: No! Don't say it!

(Carousel lights and loud bouncy music.)

CARNIE 2: Come on, come on, come on, you can do better than that!

CARNIE 1: How did pretty Holly die? Who will be the next to try?

(Triangle ding.)

MITCHELL *(with rising emotion)*: She was raped. And strangled. And—

(Lightning.)

EMMA: No! I won't let you!

CARNIE 2: Not good enough!

CARNIE 1: Say more! Say more! What have we been waiting for?

(Triangle ding.)

MITCHELL: She was raped. And strangled with a length of white rope. And he cut off—

(Lightning.)

EMMA: No!

MEREDITH: Shut up, mom! This doesn't just belong to you!

MITCHELL: He cut off her—

(Lightning. EMMA cries out and falls. Mitchell and MEREDITH freeze, then slump. The triangle dings more and more rapidly. Beginning as whispers and increasing in volume and intensity, voices chant all the rhymes about Brian Mahoney that we've heard throughout, maybe add new ones.)

VOICES: Ho, ho, hey, hey, Brian Mahoney dies today! Hey, hey, hi, hi, Brian Mahoney's gonna fry! Hey, hey, whaddaya know, Brian Mahoney's gotta go!

(MEREDITH joins in the chanting, at first playfully, then increasingly wild. EMMA and MITCHELL move around the stage and the theater. The carousel lights and music speed up, and the midway becomes increasingly surreal. Lightning flashes and strikes sporadically. Everything builds to bedlam. Then sudden silence and darkness

except for the carousel lights and music, which now are almost dreamy.)

MEREDITH *(like a jumprope chant)*: An eye for an eye! Mahoney must fry! A head for a head! We want him dead! A nose for a nose! Mahoney goes! A tooth for a tooth! We all know the truth!

(Gong strikes three o'clock.)

VOICES: Three!

FORTUNE TELLER *(offstage)*: Five small dollahs, I tell how Holly died. Such a deal. Five small dollahs, I say it for you.

(MITCHELL and MEREDITH hold aloft a huge play-money bill.)

EMMA: Don't. Don't say it. You'll kill them.

FORTUNE TELLER *(offstage)*: Whatever I get paid to see, I see.

EMMA: How would you know how she—?

MITCHELL *(holding up another bill)*: Come on. Do your stuff.

MEREDITH: We're waiting here.

FORTUNE TELLER *(offstage)*: Ooh, missy and mistah, for you I have a *good* story. Not a happy story, not a nice story or an easy story, but a verrry good story.

MITCHELL: Spare us the patter. Take your best shot.

EMMA: Mitchell, Meredith, what are you doing? Why are you putting yourselves through this?

MITCHELL: Don't you think it's about time?

MEREDITH: Get out of the way, Mom!

EMMA: After all I've gone through for you—

MITCHELL *(to FORTUNE TELLER)*: What are you waiting for? More money? You want more money? Fine. Here.

(He tosses handfuls of play money into the air, around the stage, into the audience.)

FORTUNE TELLER *(offstage)*: Hey, hey, sonny, just hold your horses. I gotta get in tune with the spirit world, know what I'm sayin'? Quiet, please! Yo! Qui-et! *(All sounds stop.)* Can't hear myself think!

(Pause. Gong strikes four o'clock.)

VOICES *(whispering)*: Four.

FORTUNE TELLER *(offstage)*: Oh, yeah, I see. Holly hitchin'. Where? Wait, wait, there's a street sign—aha! The corner of 20th and Avondale. Am I good or what? A pickup truck is slowing down. Hey, dude, what do you think *you're* lookin' at? Wait, wait, maybe I can see what kinda truck. Red. It's red. It's a ford. Late-model red Ford truck. What'd I tell you? The spirit world would have to get up early in the mornin' to put somethin' over on me.

MITCHELL: That was in the papers. The red Ford truck.

FORTUNE TELLER (*offstage*): Oh, yeah? Was the yarn doll hangin' from the rearview mirror in the papers? Hmmm? With button eyes? Hey, sonny, I'm talkin' to you. Was it?

MITCHELL: No. I don't think so. Not that I saw. Maybe I missed it—

FORTUNE TELLER (offstage): Ha! Okay, so stay with me here. Holly waves. The red Ford truck keeps goin'. Holly flips it off. She gives up. She can take the bus, but the bus is bo-ring. She starts to walk to the bus stop. The red pickup truck goes around the block and pulls up beside her again. The driver leans across the seat and opens the door for her. He's short, fair-skinned, you know that white-blond hair? And eyes so dark blue they're almost purple, almost violet, indigo. He says...

MITCHELL: Goin' my way?

FORTUNE TELLER (*offstage*): Exactly. And Holly says?

MITCHELL (*showing emotion*): Holly says, my daughter, my little girl says—

MEREDITH: I'm on my way to work at Ten Oaks Mall.

FORTUNE TELLER (*offstage*): Very good. And he says? Brian Joseph Mahoney says?

MITCHELL: I'm not heading that way. Thought I'd play hooky and spend the day in the mountains. You could come, too.

FORTUNE TELLER (*offstage*): You know, you got a knack for this. Keep goin', you're on a roll.

MITCHELL: And Holly says—

MITCHELL and EMMA: No thanks, I'll catch the bus.

FORTUNE TELLER (*offstage*): No sir. Holly says?

MITCHELL (*rising emotion*): Holly says—

MEREDITH: Why not?

MITCHELL: And gets—into—the—truck.

(*Lightning all around. EMMA cries out and staggers, revealing a huge new wound. Mitchell tends to EMMA.)*

MEREDITH: So then what?

MITCHELL: That's enough.

EMMA: Please, let's go home.

MEREDITH: But the party's not over!

EMMA: I don't think I can take any more.

CARNIE 2: Last call, ladies and gentlemen! Just a few more minutes!

VOICES: Ten. Nine. Eight.

(CARNIVAL CHARACTERS cavort. Carousel music gets wilder. Lights swirl.)

CARNIE 1: Hoo, hi, ho, hey! Brian Mahoney's on his way!

MEREDITH: This is supposed to make me feel how?

VOICES: Seven. Six.

CARNIE 1: All right! Let's wind this thing up!

VOICES: Five. Four. Fry day fry day fry day fry day! Three. Two. Fry day fry day fry day! One! *(loud frying sound.)* Hurray! That's it! He's dead! Hoooo-eee! He's dead! *(Beat.)*

MEREDITH: Yeah! And!

MITCHELL: It didn't work.

EMMA: It's over. Please, let's go home now.

MEREDITH: Talk about a let-down.

MITCHELL: What a gyp.

EMMA: Please.

FORTUNE TELLER: Tell ya what. Five small dollahs, I tell you Holly's story. One of Holly's stories.

MITCHELL: Sorry, I've got nothing to spare.

MEREDITH: I didn't bring my purse. Didn't think I'd need any money.

FORTUNE TELLER: You just haul your sorry asses over here and let's do this. No charge. C'mon, c'mon, c'mon, time's a-wastin'. *(Beat. Mitchell moves downstage and sits on the edge of the stage.)* Okey-dokey. Here we go.

EMMA: Please, please don't do this. It'll be too much for me.

(Sudden complete silence and darkness except for lightning. For the following monologue, FORTUNE TELLER drops the fake accent.)

FORTUNE TELLER: Early on the morning of October 4, 1998, sixteen-year-old Holly Emma Sundstrom was going to work at Pizza Pavilian where she'd just learned to toss a thin crust. Waiting for the #34 bus at the corner of 20th and Avondale, she chatted with the two other people who waited there every weekday morning. The bus wasn't late, the other passengers were friendly, but Holly got impatient. She stuck out her thumb. A late-model red Ford pickup truck slowed down and the blond-haired driver took a look at her. When he sped up and went on by, Holly shouted after it, "Have a nice day!" And flipped him off, and the other two bus passengers warned her about the dangers of hitchhiking. *(Dim moving spot up on MEREDITH suggesting the carousel.)* The truck circled the block and pulled into the bus stop. The driver leaned across the seat and opened the door. Holly and the other two people waiting for the bus all noticed his white-blond hair and his eyes so dark blue they were almost indigo, almost purple. He asked where she was headed, she told him, he said he was going to the mountains, and she got in. The red truck sped off. One of the others got part of his license number, 76i or maybe j, as their bus pulled up.

(Dim spot up on MITCHELL, starting to take off his clothes to reveal more underneath.) There was a yarn doll with button eyes hanging from the rearview mirror. He said a friend gave it to him. On the floor was a trigonometry book with homework folded inside the cover, a girl's name on it. He said it belonged to a friend. He had a copper bracelet around his right wrist. He said it was a gift from a friend. Holly told him to let her out at the next corner. He said he had other plans. She tried to open the door and jump out in the middle of the interstate, but he had all the doors locked.

(EMMA drifts around the stage. Lightning follows her, small bright flashes.) Holly tried everything she could think of. When she reached for the steering wheel, he backhanded her and bloodied her nose. When she pretended to flirt with him, he called her a filthy little cunt. When she cried, he pulled over to the side of the road and took her in his arms and kissed her long and hard and whispered lovingly in her ear that he was going to kill her. Rape her and kill her and dump her body in a creek.

(MITCHELL has uncovered himself to a bottom layer of

flesh-colored body stocking—or maybe even nakedness. MEREDITH is turning in circles as if on the carousel. EMMA wanders from one to the other, in and out of their spots.)

They drove for another two hours before they got to Brian Mahoney's place. The place he'd used before and would use again. A beautiful place, high up a narrow canyon, with a cool clear stream and a little cave. Holly tried to run the instant he opened the door, but he grabbed her and carried her into the cave. He raped her again and again, punching and slapping and strangling and kissing her all the time. She was screaming. She was bleeding. He put his hands around her throat and his mouth against hers and he pressed down until she wasn't breathing anymore, and he raped her again. Then he cut off her breasts, one after the other, and her hands, one after the other, and he took these four parts of Holly Emma Sundstrom with him as mementoes of the time they shared together, and he rolled her body down the hill and into the cool, clear stream.

(Huge lightning. EMMA shrieks.)
MEREDITH (wailing): Holly!
MITCHELL: Oh, God, Holly!
EMMA: I can't! I can't! I'm full!
(Lightning all around. EMMA falls. Beat.)
FORTUNE TELLER: So now you know.

SCENE SEVEN

Living room lit by ongoing lightning. EMMA is on the couch, MEREDITH and MITCHELL in chairs flanking her. Throughout the scene, CARNIE 1, CARNIE 2, FORTUNE TELLER, AND CARNIVAL CHARACTERS move far upstage, far downstage, and through the audience carrying pieces of the carnival set. The carnival is over, and they are just ordinary workers now, breaking it down, getting ready to leave town.

MEREDITH and MITCHELL are openly grieving. Examples: Sometimes they cry silently, sometimes audibly. They look at photo albums or push the albums away. MEREDITH has the huge ball or stuffed animal Holly won for her at a carnival; sometimes she holds it, sometimes it sits at her feet; sometimes she takes it offstage and then retrieves it. MITCHELL has Holly's collection of bright pretty objects—rocks, Mardi Gras beads, etc.—which he stares at, plays with, puts away, takes out again.

MITCHELL and MEREDITH tend to EMMA, smoothing her hair, checking her temperature with a hand to the forehead, tucking the blanket around her, talking softly to her. MITCHELL gives her medicine with water. MEREDITH puts salve on her wounds. This is a quiet, sad, tender scene showing the beginning of healing.

FORTUNE TELLER *(no accent, carrying last large piece of carnival set across stage)*: Now. Now I can see into your future.

Lights down.

END OF PLAY

STRAIGHT SITTING

A PLAY IN TWO ACTS

Production History

Straight Sitting had staged readings at the following venues:
2009, Colorado Theatre Guild, New Ventures, Denver, CO
2011, The Edge Theater: On Your Feet, Lakewood, CO
It was a finalist in the 2012, The Edge Theater: On the Edge
New Plays Festival, Lakewood, CO

Characters

ALEX HAHN, boy with extensive history of abuse and neglect, adopted two years ago. He maintains an allegiance to his birthmother while desperately wanting and desperately fighting closeness with his adoptive mother.

MADLYN CAREY and ROSS CAREY, age 45-55, husband-and-wife team of psychotherapists internationally known for their work with children with reactive attachment disorder, genuinely dedicated but have bought into their own mythos. Very much in love with each other, passionate about their work.

STEPHANIE VARGAS, late twenties, graduate student intern with the Careys, whom she reveres.

KATHY HAHN, late forties, ALEX's adoptive mother, corporate executive, accustomed to being self-sufficient and in charge, terrified for and sometimes of her son.

SAM HAHN, early seventies, KATHY's father, retired police officer, skeptical of mental health therapy, becoming close to Alex.

JASMINE SIMMONS, mid-twenties, ALEX's birthmother, abusive and neglectful but fiercely bonded to her son whom Social Services has taken away, pregnant and will likely lose this baby as well because she's still drugging.

ROGER LaFOND, any adult age, any race, possible birthfather of ALEX, not abusive but not very involved, has a distant fondness for the idea of having a son.

BRODY HUMES, any adult age, any race, possible birthfather of ALEX, physically abused him.

QUENTIN McALLISTER, any adult age, any race, possible birthfather of ALEX, sexually molested him.

CHORUS MEMBERS of PARENTS and CHILDREN (The same actors may be cast as BRODY, QUENTIN, CHORUS MEMBERS and PARENTS/CHILDREN.)

Settings

All present day:
Room in Kathy's house
Campsite at night
Therapy rooms divided by an observation window mirrored on one side
Waiting room
The Careys' office
The Careys' bedroom
Spectator benches in a courtroom

ACT I

SCENE ONE

Dark stage. We hear ALEX raging. This is no ordinary tantrum, but full-blown, out-of-control fury. Most of it is wordless and primal, but sometimes what he says is clear.

ALEX: I hate you! I'm gonna kill you! I'm gonna kill myself!
(More raging, screaming, crying, breaking things. Then a beat of silence.)

SCENE TWO

Downstage spot up on a straight-back chair. STEPHANIE enters, sits very straight and still on the chair.

STEPHANIE: Alexander Michael Samuel Simmons Hahn. A child dangerous to himself and others. But not lost. Not yet. Ross and MADLYN Carey taught that if we could be strong enough, if Alex and the rest of us could be brave enough, there was still hope. For him and for the world.
(Spot down.)

SCENE THREE

Lights up on CAREYS' office where STEPHANIE is interviewing for an internship with ROSS and MADLYN CAREY.

STEPHANIE: —most of what both of you have written about—on the topic of reactive attachment disorder, and I find it—fascinating.

MADYLN: Have you ever experienced a significant loss yourself, Stephanie?

STEPHANIE: I—I don't think so. My grandparents died when I was little, and I remember being sad, but it didn't traumatize me or anything. *(Beat.)* Sorry. *(MADLYN makes a note.)* Does that—will that count against me for the internship?

MADYLN: What do you know about your birth?

STEPHANIE: Um, I don't—*(brightens.)* Oh, I was a preemie. *(MADLYN nods, makes a note.)* Is that good?

(They all laugh, STEPHANIE a bit nervously.)

I think I was in the hospital for a while before they could take me home. *(MADLYN makes a note.)*

ROSS: As part of the training we would expect you to experience the straight-sitting and rebirthing techniques yourself.

STEPHANIE: Cool.

ROSS: It can bring up all sorts of stuff.

MADYLN: Which is the point. We don't have the right to inflict it on somebody else if we haven't faced our own shit.

STEPHANIE: You've both done it?

MADYLN: Every once in a while. Renews us, keeps us honest. And we invite other professionals and students to observe, for training purposes.

ROSS: Your trauma was pre-verbal, before conscious memory, so—

STEPHANIE: My trauma?

ROSS: Prematurity, parental abandonment—

STEPHANIE: My parents didn't abandon me!

ROSS: Being in the hospital away from them would have felt like abandonment to baby Stephanie.

STEPHANIE: I've never felt abandoned or traumatized. My life is actually pretty boring.

ROSS: Nobody's life is boring. Everybody has a history.

MADYLN: It's a miracle anybody attaches to anybody.

(ROSS and MADLYN exchange smiles.)

ROSS: But we do.

MADYLN: Yes. We do.

STEPHANIE: I want to do this, if you'll have me.

SCENE FOUR

Spot up on KATHY's living room where KATHY is in a rocking chair holding ALEX like a baby and singing a lullaby to him. He is swaddled in a blanket and sucking his thumb. SAM enters.

SAM: He's not a baby.
KATHY: Dad. Hush.
ALEX: Hi, Grandpa!
KATHY: Alex. Hush.
SAM: He's too big for that.
KATHY: Alex and I didn't get to do baby things when he was a baby, did we, Alex?
SAM: With some things we don't get a second chance.
KATHY: People who know better than you or me say this isn't one of them.
SAM: You ask me—
(KATHY shushes him, finishes the lullaby, holds ALEX close for a moment, kisses him, then begins to unwrap the blanket.)
KATHY: Okay, Alex, Grandpa's here.
SAM: Go look in the garage, Alex. I brought you a surprise.
KATHY: Dad?
ALEX: What is it?
SAM: Go look. *(ALEX exits.)*
KATHY: What is it?
SAM: Every kid needs a dog.
KATHY: You got him a dog? Without talking to me first?
SAM: A pup. The people down the street had six to get rid of.
KATHY: The last thing I need is more pee and poop to clean up.
SAM: He's still doing that?
KATHY: In his closet. I thought we were past that months ago. All down the wall. In his shoes.
SAM: Hell, Kathy, why do you put up with that foolishness?
KATHY: I don't just "put up with it." He had to help clean it up. He has to do extra chores to pay me back for the new shoes.

But I'm told it's not unusual with these kids.

SAM: Never get anywhere in this world acting like a damn baby.

KATHY: That's why he's been learning straight sitting.

SAM: What kind of new age hogwash is that?

KATHY: It's a technique in attachment therapy. Kind of like meditation, only more so. He has to sit up straight and still. It's to help him learn self-control and focus, so he can function in the world. Like you said.

SAM: I didn't need cockamamie "techniques" to learn that, and neither did you.

KATHY: He's been traumatized.

SAM: Everybody's got problems. Everybody's got a past. Not everybody craps in the closet.

KATHY: Not everybody was left alone all night at two years old. Not everybody was burned with cigarettes. Not everybody was raped before he even had words to tell about it. *(Beat.)*

SAM: I didn't know.

KATHY: Maybe I shouldn't have told you.

SAM: Jesus.

KATHY: Don't think less of him.

SAM: Why would I think less of *him*? Somebody better be in jail.

KATHY: I don't know.

SAM: He's a good kid.

KATHY: Yes, he is.

SAM: And a great little hiker. Knows his trees and plants pretty good, if I do say so myself.

KATHY: He's sweet and smart and funny. But he's scared to death. And furious. Who could blame him?

SAM: Well, after two years he oughta know he won't get hurt here.

KATHY: The way it's been explained to me is that he is starting to trust me and love me—and you, too, grandpa—and that's why things are getting worse. He's fighting it off.

SAM: That makes no damn sense.

KATHY: But neither does what happened to him.

SAM: God damn.

KATHY: I know.

SAM: Well, but that was then. This is now. It does the boy no good to make excuses for him.

KATHY: I'm doing everything I know to do. I just hope I can be a good enough mother for him.

SAM: The dog'll stay at my house. He can take care of it. Learn responsibility.

KATHY: He's nowhere near ready for that, dad. We've got lots of re-parenting work to do first.

SAM: Psychobabble, if you ask me.

KATHY: Which I didn't. Our therapists say—

SAM: Your therapist is full of shit. If you ask me.

KATHY: Actually, dad, we're working with Ross and MADLYN Carey. They're experts in reactive attachment disorder. They have some pretty innovative techniques that have helped a lot of kids and parents. They're internationally recognized—

SAM: Doesn't mean they're not full of shit. Not to mention what I bet they charge. And how do you know those kids wouldn't have gotten better anyway?

KATHY: Dad, please. I'm really scared for him. He's—he's been setting fires, too.

SAM: Yeah, well, that's pretty normal. Like we used to say on the job, show me a house fire and I'll show you a kid with matches.

KATHY: It can also mean serious problems. Especially combined with the other stuff. I don't know what else to do.

SAM: Maybe there's nothing to do.

KATHY: There has to be. *(ALEX enters.)*

ALEX: Mom! Guess what? Grandpa got me a puppy!

KATHY: I heard.

ALEX: Her name's Jasmine!

SAM: It's a male.

ALEX: Jasmine can be a boy's name.

SAM: No—

KATHY: How about we call him Jazz?

ALEX: Yeah! Jazz! Cool! Thanks, Grandpa! (ALEX *hugs* SAM *and then* KATHY.)

(Quietly to KATHY): But it's really Jasmine, okay?

KATHY: Yeah, okay.

SAM: How'd you like to go camping this weekend?

(KATHY and ALEX talk over each other.)

KATHY: Dad, we should talk about this—

ALEX: Yay, camping!

SAM *(to KATHY):* A little grandfather-grandson—what d'you call it? Attachment?

ALEX: Can we have a campfire?

KATHY: Oh, God.

SAM *(to KATHY):* Learn fire safety. *(To ALEX):* we'll bring the dog.

ALEX: Jazz.

SAM: Jazz.

ALEX: I'll go tell him! *(ALEX runs offstage.)*

SAM: I'll help.

KATHY: You better. Because I'm not taking care of a dog on top of everything else—

SAM: With the therapy thing. The attachment whatever. It'll be expensive.

KATHY: You don't have to do that. I'm the parent. I'm the one who made this commitment.

SAM: Kathy, I'm not asking you. I'll help. Financially and whatever else. I'm the grandparent. If you think these "experts" know what they're talking about, we'll go for it.

KATHY: Thanks, Dad.

SAM: We're family. The three of us.

KATHY: Yes.

SAM: Your mother would be proud.

KATHY: She'd think I was crazy.

SAM: But proud of you. *(KATHY hugs him.)*

KATHY: I better go see what he's doing. (KATHY exits. Beat.)

SAM: God damn.

(SAM exits. Lights down except for a bright spot on the straight-back chair.)

SCENE FIVE

ALEX enters, sits ramrod-straight. He is motionless and silent long enough for the audience to begin to be uncomfortable, then exits. STEPHANIE enters carrying a mannequin which she puts on the chair to sit as ALEX was.

STEPHANIE: My thesis was on reactive attachment disorder, RAD. The literature is extensive and not encouraging. These are the kids you hear about without a conscience. Empty. Soulless. So traumatized they can't care about anybody. It's terrifying, and fascinating.

(ALEX races across the stage, knocking the mannequin over. STEPHANIE sets it back in place.)

There's evidence that abuse and neglect actually change the hard-wiring of the brain and physically stunt its development.

(ALEX enters, sits on the chair with the mannequin in his lap, tosses it onto the floor and exits. STEPHANIE sets the mannequin straight in the chair again.)

Everything I could find said these are lost children who will almost certainly bring harm to themselves and to other people and to society. It made my boyfriend furious that I wanted to "waste my time" with kids like that.

(ALEX enters, throwing things at STEPHANIE and the mannequin. STEPHANIE protects the mannequin.)

Then I found the work of Ross and MADLYN Carey. There was compelling anecdotal evidence that they'd helped RAD kids everybody else had given up on. There is also growing scientific evidence that traumatized brains can heal. You can see it on the brain scan. Alex Hahn was my first case. I was going to be on the cutting edge. Part of a miracle.

MADLYN *(booming voice-over)*: Alexander Hahn! Sit up straight! You have not been excused!

(ALEX looks around, sits on the floor in the straight-sitting posture. STEPHANIE exits. ALEX picks up the mannequin and walks around with it.)

ROSS *(booming voice-over)*: Alex! You've just earned more time! Sit down! Back straight, face forward, very quiet. Now!

(ALEX glances around again, sits, places the mannequin beside him. Beat. Then he scoots backward out of the spot,

leaving the mannequin straight-sitting.)

SCENE SIX

Lights up on KATHY's living room. SAM and ALEX enter, talking. ALEX is carrying the puppy.

ALEX: I'm a good puppy trainer, huh, Grandpa?

SAM: Yep.

ALEX: She knows her name. Jasmine.

SAM: He knows *his* name's jazz. Smart dog.

ALEX *(to the puppy)*: You're such a smart dog, yes, you are.

SAM: He likes you.

ALEX: Why?

SAM: You're nice to him. You feed him and you play with him and you teach him stuff.

ALEX: Yeah. *(ALEX nuzzles the puppy.)*

SAM: When your mom gets home you can show her what you taught jazz to do.

ALEX: Grandpa?

SAM: Yeah?

ALEX: Does Jazz love me?

SAM: I don't know—dogs don't really—yeah, sure, I think he does. Love you.

ALEX: Cool! *(beat.)* Grandpa?

SAM: Yeah?

ALEX: I love Jazz.

(Lights down.)

SCENE SEVEN

Lights up dim on another part of the stage. JASMINE and ALEX enter, playing.

ALEX: Tag, Mommy, you're it!

JASMINE: You caught me this time, sweetie, fair and square!

BRODY *(offstage)*: Hey, Jasmine! Let's go, babe!

(JASMINE exits, giggling and running. ALEX exits, chasing her.

KATHY enters, hiding her eyes, playing hide-and-seek.)

KATHY: 6, 5, 4, 3, 2, 1, here I come, ready or not!

ALEX *(offstage)*: Here, Mom! I'm here! Come and find me!

KATHY: Okay, I give up! Ollyollyinfree! Alex! Come in now, it's getting dark. Alex? You're scaring me!

(ALEX enters, goes to her. BRODY and JASMINE enter, slow-dancing. They kiss, become increasingly passionate. ALEX pulls away from KATHY. KATHY exits. Carrying the mannequin, ALEX pushes himself and it between JASMINE and BRODY, who pantomimes slap-ping, kicking, pushing him.)

ALEX: Ow!

JASMINE: Brody! What are you doing? Your own son!

(She tries to protect ALEX. ALEX puts the mannequin between himself and BRODY so it takes the abuse. JASMINE pulls BRODY away and they exit. ALEX hits the mannequin several times, throws it aside, stands alone as lights fade.)

SCENE EIGHT

Lights up dim on nighttime camping. SAM and ALEX are side by side in sleeping bags by a campfire under the stars, running a small toy truck back and forth between them.

ALEX: Jazz is asleep.

SAM: 'bout time.

ALEX: I'm scared.

SAM: Nothing to be scared of. You think the dog'd sleep if there was danger?

ALEX: Scared of the dark.

SAM: Nothing in the dark that's not there in the light. Go to sleep. *(beat.)*

ALEX: Grandpa?

SAM *(long-suffering)*: Yeah.

ALEX: How come you're not a cop anymore?

SAM: Retired.

ALEX: Like you got new tires?

SAM *(chuckles)*: No, retired is when you stop working because you've had enough.

ALEX: Oh, like you're really really tired! Re-tired! Get it? *(They both laugh, ALEX more enthusiastically than SAM.)*

SAM: And you want to do something else with your life besides work.

ALEX: Like what?

SAM: Like going camping with your grandson.

ALEX: Yeah.

SAM: Aren't you sleepy? I'm sleepy. Jazz is sleepy. G'night. *(beat.)*

ALEX: Grandpa?

SAM: Huh.

ALEX: Did you used to catch bad guys?

SAM: Once in a while.

ALEX: I have to pee.

SAM: You sure?

Alex *(on his feet, increasingly urgent)*: Yeah, Grandpa, I gotta pee. *(SAM groans, extricates himself from his sleeping bag, stands.)*

SAM: Okay, come on. *(SAM and ALEX move toward exit.)*

ALEX: Where's the bathroom?

SAM: We'll just find you a tree.

ALEX: Oh, I'm not allowed to—

SAM: We won't tell your mom.

ALEX: No, I can't. It's wrong! It's dirty! I have to pee and poop in the toilet.

SAM: It's okay.

ALEX: No, it's not!

SAM: Look, kid. I was a cop for a lotta years. I'm telling you it's all right. There's no toilet close by. You have to pee. Do what you gotta do. *(ALEX hesitates, then exits. SAM waits. Then ALEX enters.)* Everything come out all right?

(ALEX doesn't get it at first. Then they both laugh and walk back toward the sleeping bags.)

ALEX: So can you still catch bad guys.

SAM: Sure.

ALEX: Good.

SAM: You got some bad guys you want caught? *(ALEX takes SAM's hand for a moment. They get back into their sleeping bags.)* Good-night.

ALEX: Night. *(Beat.)* I never went camping before.

SAM: You know, one of the things people do when they go camping is *sleep*.

ALEX: You never took me camping before.

SAM: Your mom—we didn't think it was safe yet.

ALEX: Why not?

SAM: Didn't know if you could handle it. What you might do.

ALEX: Like what?

SAM: Hurt yourself, run off or something.

(ALEX scrambles to his feet and runs off.)

ALEX *(calls over his shoulder)*: You mean like this?

(SAM struggles to get out of his sleeping bag.)

SAM: Hey! Get back here! Alex!

ALEX: Can't catch me!

SAM *(under his breath, getting out of the sleeping bag)*: Goddammit!

(Lights down.)

SCENE NINE

Lights up on KATHY in the CAREYS' waiting room, waiting for ALEX. KATHY is working on her laptop. Another PARENT enters. They acknowledge each other. Beat.

PARENT: Is your child in the follow-up group, too?

KATHY: No, he's—we're—current.

PARENT: Oh, I remember when we were where you are now.

KATHY: And now you're back? That's not a good sign, is it?

PARENT: My daughter hasn't been here for a while and it's just time for a tune-up.

KATHY: I hope I'll be able to say that someday.

PARENT: The Careys aren't for everybody, but they sure helped us.

KATHY: Good to hear. *(Beat.)* Let me ask you something, though. How do you know things wouldn't have gotten better anyway? There's no research that I can find.

PARENT: We ask ourselves that same thing. But nothing else

worked. And it's better than meds with all those side effects.

KATHY: Maybe it was the cumulative effect of all those things you tried with your daughter. Or maybe she just outgrew it.

PARENT: Maybe.

KATHY: Do you mind if I ask what she did?

PARENT: She was prostituting to get money for heroin. She was threatening our other children—

(ROSS enters.)

ROSS *(to PARENT)*: The group should be over in a few minutes. *(To KATHY)* will you join us now?

(KATHY follows ROSS into the office, turning to look at the PARENT, who is now reading a magazine and not looking at her. KATHY and ROSS exit.)

SCENE TEN

Spot up on STEPHANIE.

STEPHANIE: Ross said there might be a place for me with them. MADLYN was harder.

SCENE ELEVEN

Lights up on MADLYN, ROSS, and KATHY in the CAREYS' office watching ALEX through a one-way mirror.

STEPHANIE: I wanted it. Oh, I wanted it.
(STEPHANIE joins MADLYN and ROSS. Spot down.)
ROSS: He's a tough one.
STEPHANIE: Tougher than most?
ROSS: The self-protective instinct is pretty amazing. Especially when it's actually self-destructive.
MADYLN: Poor kid. He's fighting for his life.
KATHY: He's just sitting there.
MADYLN: Pretty effective way to fight. Just ask Gandhi.
KATHY: He looks so small and alone.

ROSS: He is small. That's why there's hope.

MADYLN: And he is alone.

KATHY: He is not alone!

ROSS: He's unattached. That's about as alone as you can get.

KATHY: But I love him so much. And sometimes he loves me.

MADYLN: To him right now that love feels life-threatening.

ROSS: Like if he loves you he'll die. When in fact it's quite the opposite. He'll die if he *doesn't* love.

KATHY: He'll really die?

ROSS: Spiritually and psychologically at least.

MADYLN: People have been known to literally stop living when they can't attach.

ROSS: That's why we're all here.

KATHY: This seems so harsh.

MADYLN: We have to be stronger than he is. Especially you. And his fear makes him incredibly strong.

(ROSS pushes a button and his voice booms.)

ROSS: Alexander Hahn! Sit up straight! *(KATHY flinches.)*

KATHY: Maybe I'm being selfish. I've always been so close to my own parents.

STEPHANIE: I read that in your adoption home study.

MADYLN: We were glad to see that. It's something we look for.

KATHY: That's what I want to have with my son.

ROSS: But it's a two-edged sword, like everything else in this work. If the adoptive parent can't accept anything but their ideal parent-child relationship, we're in trouble.

KATHY: So, if I'm close to my parents you worry, and if I'm not close to my parents you worry.

ROSS: Pretty much. *(Laughter.)*

MADYLN: We all need to realize this could be the last chance for Alex.

KATHY: Oh, I can't believe—

MADYLN: Fire-setting. Smearing feces. Hours-long rages.

STEPHANIE: Classic symptoms.

KATHY: But he's so young.

MADYLN: The stakes are very high. For him and for you and for society.

KATHY: My poor little boy. *(In tears, KATHY excuses herself with a gesture and exits.)*

MADYLN: I hope she can stay with it. A lot of parents can't. These kids are scared and scary.

STEPHANIE: It's no wonder, considering what they've been through.

ROSS: These were survival skills for him. But now they're not working.

MADYLN: Ain't it a bitch? You think you know how to live in this world, and then you don't.

STEPHANIE: I've noticed that. *(Laughter.)* I guess you must get used to all the awful stories.

MADYLN: You can't ever let yourself get used to them. *(MADLYN presses the button and speaks into the mic.)* Alex! Pay attention!

STEPHANIE: What was he doing?

MADYLN: Dissociating. Going somewhere else in his head. Often our kids will do that when they perceive something as dangerous or traumatic.

ROSS: Such as being asked to let themselves feel close to another human being.

STEPHANIE: So now what?

MADYLN: Ross and I will consult. We have a whole bag of tricks.

STEPHANIE: Well, if anybody can help him, you guys can.

ROSS: Some we haven't been able to. But we're always learning and refining our techniques.

MADYLN: And gaining courage. Finding ways to give courage to our children and parents.

(ROSS stands behind her and puts his hands on her shoulders.)

ROSS: It takes courage to live a life, a human life.

MADYLN: Stephanie, would you go talk to Kathy?

STEPHANIE: Sure. Let me find my notes—

MADYLN: No notes. Taking notes dilutes your attention.

STEPHANIE: How do you remember? There's so much going on.

MADYLN: If you're giving them the attention they deserve, remembering isn't a problem. Forgetting can be a problem.

STEPHANIE: But I'm not as good as you. Maybe one day I will be—what should I say to her?

ROSS: Just support her that she's doing the right thing for her son.

MADYLN: That we know what we're doing.

STEPHANIE: I could remind her that you're world-renowned for all the kids you've helped and that's why I'm interning here.

ROSS: It's the work that matters. Not personalities. *(STEPHANIE exits. ROSS and MADLYN stand, put their arms around each other, watch ALEX through the one-way mirror.)* What is it now, about thirty minutes?

MADYLN: Thirty-two.

MADLYN and ROSS *(booming)*: Alexander Hahn! Sit up straight!

(Lights down. Pause.)

SCENE TWELVE

Then flames, starting as a small glow in one corner, then spreading until the entire stage is firelit. ALEX runs across the stage, whooping. Firelight fades. Dark stage.

SCENE THIRTEEN

Spot up on mannequin straight-sitting. KATHY enters.

KATHY: Hi, Alex. How ya doing, sweetheart? *(KATHY kneels beside the mannequin, takes it in her arms.)* I love you, son. I love you so much. *(KATHY looks up.)* I'm just not sure about this—

MADLYN *(booming voice-over)*: Remember, Kathy, he meant to burn the house down.

(KATHY gently lays the mannequin down, places a pillow on each side, and lies on the pillows across the mannequin.)

KATHY: Is this right?

ROSS *(booming voice-over)*: That's it, Kathy, you're doing fine.

ALEX *(offstage)*: I can't breathe! You're too heavy!

KATHY: He says he can't breathe.

ROSS: Don't you buy into that! Stay the course, Kathy! (*Pause.*)

MADYLN: Okay, Kathy. Talk to your infant son.

KATHY (*awkwardly*): My baby. My sweet little baby. Mommy's so glad to have you. Mommy's so glad to have her sweet little baby boy. (*Pause.*)

MADLYN (*prompting*): Have you waited all your life for this, Kathy?

KATHY: I've waited all my life for you, Alex. All my life I've wanted a little boy just like you. I'll always love you. I'll always keep you safe—

Alex (*offstage*): Get off me! You're heavy!

KATHY: He says I'm too heavy.

ROSS, MADLYN, and STEPHANIE (*booming voice-over*): No! Don't move! Stay where you are!

(Long pause. Lights stay up, dim.)

SCENE FOURTEEN

Spot up on JASMINE holding baby ALEX, perhaps as a doll or in pantomime.

JASMINE (*singing*): Hush, little Alex, don't say a word. Mama's gonna buy you a mockingbird—

(*QUENTIN enters, grabs JASMINE, pulls her to him for a rough kiss. She drops the baby.*)

The baby! Quentin, you hurt our baby!

(*QUENTIN picks up the baby and shoves him back into her arms, then exits. JASMINE lays the baby down on the ground again and runs after QUENTIN.*)

Quentin, baby, wait! I'm sorry! I didn't mean it! He's okay! I'm sorry!

(Spot down. The baby cries.)

SCENE FIFTEEN

KATHY (singing): If that mockingbird don't sing, Mama's gonna buy you a diamond ring—MADLYN (*booming voice-over*):

All right, Kathy. Now I want you to go sit in the rocking chair. *(KATHY doesn't move.)* Kathy.

(KATHY half-rises, kisses the mannequin, goes to the rocking chair.)

Now, little baby Alex, crawl to your mama. *(Pause.)* Alex. Crawl to your new mama like a baby. *(ALEX enters, crawls to KATHY, stops.)* Get up into her lap. Kathy, help him. Pick him up if you can.

(With ALEX lying in her lap like a baby, KATHY wraps him in a blanket, leaving his head uncovered, and rocks him.)

ROSS: Yes. Yes, that's beautiful. Now the bottle. *(KATHY feeds ALEX from a baby bottle.)* Yes.

STEPHANIE *(moved to tears)*: God, that is beautiful.

MADYLN: Now, Mama, look into your son's eyes. Alex, look into your mama's eyes. *(long pause.)*

KATHY *(sobbing)*: Oh, Alex, I'm so proud of you! I love you so much.

ROSS: He's doing it! He's actually making contact!

MADYLN and ROSS: Yay, Alex! Good for you!

(Applause. STEPHANIE gets to her feet, clapping enthusiastically. Lights down.)

SCENE SIXTEEN

Lights up on another part of the stage where JASMINE is playing with a big bright ball. ALEX runs to play with her; they are happy, laughing, affectionate with each other. Then JASMINE accidentally throws the ball offstage.

JASMINE: Oh, I'm sorry, honey! I'm such a klutz!

ALEX *(chases the ball)*: Don't worry, Mom, I'll get it!

JASMINE: I'll be right here, son! You're such a little man! *(ROGER enters.)*

ROGER: Hey, Jasmine.

JASMINE: Roger, baby, come play with us. That boy of yours is an athlete, just like his daddy.

(ROGER and JASMINE toss another, smaller ball back and forth, JASMINE squealing in delight.)

ALEX: Wait for me, Mom! I'm looking for our ball.

JASMINE: I'm not going anyplace, sweetie. We're not going anyplace, are we, roger?

ROGER: Nossir, we're staying right here, son. Your mom and me's just having fun.

(ROGER and JASMINE toss the small ball a few more times while continuing to talk.)

JASMINE: He gets scared when I leave.

ROGER: Can't blame him.

JASMINE: Sometimes I got no choice but to leave, y'know?

ROGER: You do the best you can, jasmine. Whole town knows that.

JASMINE: Whole town except him. Except Alex. *(One of them misses and it goes offstage. JASMINE can't find it. ROGER exits.)* Roger? Where are you going? Please don't go!

ALEX: Oh, here it is! I found it, Mom!

JASMINE *(to both ROGER and ALEX)*: Sorry, I'm sorry, I didn't mean to.

(JASMINE exits. Lights down.)

SCENE SEVENTEEN

ALEX crosses into the therapy room, carrying the large ball.

ALEX: Mom, I found our ball. Mom?

MADYLN: You can't stop her, Alex. You're just a little kid.

ROSS: Give it up, Alex. It's not your fault. It's not your job to make her stay.

ALEX *(jumping up and down and bouncing the ball)*: Mom mom mom mom mom.

STEPHANIE: Alexander Hahn, sit still!

MADYLN: Good, Stephanie.

(ALEX tries to crawl on top of the ball, falls off, cries.)

ALEX: Mom mom mom mom mom mom.

(KATHY enters, tries to hug ALEX.)

KATHY: I'm here, Alex. Mommy's here.

ALEX *(inconsolable)*: Mom mom mom mom mom.

MADYLN: That's it, Kathy. Hold him tight.

STEPHANIE: He doesn't want her. He won't even look at her. Are you sure—

ROSS: It's not as simple as wanting or not wanting. It's both and neither.

(ALEX allows himself to be held, then clings to KATHY.)

ALEX: Mommy.

STEPHANIE: Oh! Look at that!

JASMINE *(off-stage)*: I'm your real mother, Alex. I'll always be your real mother.

(ALEX wrenches himself free of KATHY, striking out at her, and runs across the stage. KATHY catches him.)

ALEX: Let me go!

KATHY: I won't ever let you go!

(ALEX rages, long and hard. KATHY holds on, crooning.)

ALEX: Let go of me! I hate you! I'll kill you!

STEPHANIE: I've never seen anything like this.

MADYLN: Hang on, Kathy! We can't let him win this one!

ROSS: He's got to know you're stronger than he is.

KATHY: I won't let you hurt me, Alex. I'll keep you safe.

(Finally, ALEX collapses in her arms. She sits on the floor with him in her lap, rocking and crooning. Spot up on STEPHANIE.)

STEPHANIE: To teach a hurt child how to love and be loved. To create a family. To make a difference in the world that will affect generations. Nothing seemed more important than that.

(Spot down.)

SCENE EIGHTEEN

Lights up on KATHY's living room.

ALEX *(walking backward, giving the hand signal for "stay" to the puppy offstage)*: Good boy, Jazz, good dog! Stay! You stay! Good dog! *(ALEX exits toward the puppy. Offstage, giggling and squealing, playing with Jazz.)* Here's your treat, Jazz! You're such a good boy!

(Lights down.)

SCENE NINETEEN

Lights up on the CAREYS' office. MADLYN is working at the computer. ROSS enters, upset.

ROSS: Hey, remember Lisa Hildebrandt?

MADYLN: Natasha's mom. Sure. What's wrong?

ROSS: Natasha tried to kill her.

MADYLN: What?

ROSS: Locked her in the bathroom and set the house on fire.

MADYLN: How did you hear—it's been, what, ten years since she consulted with us—

ROSS: Greg emailed me.

MADYLN: Did they do attachment work with Greg?

ROSS: He just heard about it, thought we'd want to know.

(MADLYN goes to ROSS. They hold each other.)

MADYLN: Maybe we could have—if Lisa'd decided—

ROSS: Who knows?

MADYLN: We can't save them all.

ROSS: Poor Natasha. She was one screwed-up kid. Scary even then. *(pause.)*

MADYLN: Poor Lisa. *(Pause.)*

(Lights down.)

SCENE TWENTY

Dim spot up on scenes depicting successful therapeutic "rebirthing" in bright colors and dance-like motion: CHILDREN emerging from blankets into the arms of their new PARENTS, cries like those of newborn babies, PARENTS joyously calling their CHILDREN's names as if naming them for the first time.

PARENT 1: Elizabeth! Elizabeth, you are so beautiful!

PARENT 2: Christopher!

PARENT 3: We've waited so long for you!

PARENT 4 and 5: My baby. My sweet little baby. My sweet little baby boy.

PARENT 6: Marisol! Marisol. I'm here!

PARENT 7: You're safe! Welcome home!

(STEPHANIE dances on the periphery, wanting to join in but not knowing how, finally exits.)

SCENE TWENTY-ONE

Lights up on KATHY in the rocking chair with ALEX in her lap like a baby. SAM enters, carrying a small bundle wrapped in a blanket.

SAM: Alex, go to your room.

KATHY: Dad!

SAM: Alex! Go to your room!

(ALEX exits.)

KATHY: What—?

SAM *(holding out the bundle)*: Jazz is dead.

KATHY: Oh, no, Alex loves that puppy!

SAM: I think Alex killed him.

KATHY: Why do you think—? He wouldn't—

SAM: The body was wrapped up in that new red jacket I just got him and put in the trash can under other stuff. I bet he was going to say he ran away.

KATHY: That doesn't mean he killed him. He could have just—or if he did, it had to have been an accident—

SAM: His neck's been broken, Kathy. Wrung. Like you'd kill a chicken.

(Lights down.)

SCENE TWENTY-TWO

Lights up on the therapy room where MADLYN, ROSS, and STEPHANIE are talking.

STEPHANIE: —one screwed-up little kid. That thing with the puppy is really creepy.

MADYLN: A lot of times things get worse before they get better. Kids will make a last-ditch stand.

ROSS: And so will we.

STEPHANIE: I love the concept of having to fight to claim your life.

MADYLN: Talk's cheap. Put your body where your mouth is.

ROSS: If you're ready. It's early in your internship. You can just observe this one if you want to.

STEPHANIE: I'm not here to observe.

MADYLN: Atta girl.

ROSS: But if she's not ready—

MADYLN: Is any of us ever ready? Is Alex ready? Would he say he's ready?

ROSS: Alex is an emergency.

MADYLN: Ross, if she's going to do this work—

ROSS: I'm just saying—

STEPHANIE: I'm ready.

(STEPHANE sits on the floor. Lights up dim on the other side of the observation mirror, where parents from earlier scenes are observing.)

MADYLN: Don't take this lightly, Stephanie. Don't play with this.

STEPHANIE: I'm serious. I'm ready.

MADYLN: All right! I'm proud of you.

(ROSS and MADLYN spread a blanket on the floor. STEPHANIE crawls onto it and lies down in a fetal position. They wrap it around her, swaddling her snugly, draping her face lightly. One of them at her head and the other at her feet, they stroke her.)

MADLYN *(crooning)*: How's it feel in there, little baby?

PARENT 2: Little baby, little baby Stephanie.

STEPHANIE: Warm. Dark.

PARENT 4: Warm and dark. Warm and dark and safe.

MADLYN: Warm and dark and safe. What else?

STEPHANIE: Safe. Tight. Safe.

ROSS: Stephanie, are you ready to be born into the world?

MADYLN: Ross, that's not long enough. She needs to know what it's really like.

STEPHANIE: It's nice in here.

PARENT 6: It's nice in there before you're born.

PARENT 5: But you can't stay.

PARENT 3: It's not life.

ROSS: You can't stay in there forever, baby Stephanie. You have to come out into the world.

STEPHANIE: Why?

ROSS: If you stayed in there forever, you'd die.

MADYLN: You've got to fight to claim your life. It takes courage.

STEPHANIE: Maybe I don't want to. Maybe I like it in here.

(ROSS and MADLYN exchange knowing looks, then increase

their pressure on STEPHANIE through the blanket.)

ROSS: Can you feel that, Stephanie? Can you feel the pressure to be born?

PARENT 6: The invitation to be born?

STEPHANIE: I feel it!

MADLYN: The world wants you, Stephanie. Life is calling.

(They press harder. STEPHANIE groans.)

STEPHANIE: It hurts!

MADYLN: Yes. Being born hurts. Being alive hurts.

STEPHANIE: I can't breathe!

ROSS: Fight, Steffie! Fight for air!

PARENT 1: She can't breathe!

PARENT 3: Watch out!

MADYLN: Come on, little baby, push!

ROSS: Come on out!

PARENT 2: She's breathing!

(STEPHANIE pushes her way free and out into their arms. Tears, cheers, rejoicing from the three of them and from the PARENTS. Lights down except mannequin's spot. PARENTS and CHILDREN circle the mannequin, then exit, leaving the mannequin straight-sitting alone in the spot for several beats.)

SCENE TWENTY-THREE

Lights up on STEPHANIE, MADLYN, and ROSS in the CAREYS' office a few minutes later.

STEPHANIE: That was incredible!

ROSS: It's just the beginning. But it is a beginning.

STEPHANIE: To be present at that moment. Like being an alchemist.

ROSS: It is a rush.

STEPHANIE: I want to do that. I want my life to be about making a safe place for hurt kids to love and be loved. Like yours.

ROSS: Understanding, of course, that loving and being loved isn't safe, any place, any time, for any of us.

STEPHANIE: Oh, come on. Why do you say that?

ROSS: One way or another, we'll all lose everyone we love. That's the human condition.

STEPHANIE: You know what? That's not exactly what I want to hear at this point in my life.

(STEPHANIE shows her engagement ring. MADLYN hugs her.)

ROSS: Congratulations. That's wonderful. I'm a big fan of marriage.

STEPHANIE: How long have you been married?

ROSS: Coming up on twenty-five years.

STEPHANIE: And it's good?

MADLYNE and ROSS: Yes.

STEPHANIE: So, what was all that about losing everybody we love?

ROSS: Either they will leave us, or we will leave them.

MADYLN: Unless we happen to die at exactly the same instant.

ROSS: We can always hope.

(ROSS and MADLYN laugh.)

STEPHANIE: God, that's so cynical.

ROSS: Stephanie, we are probably the least cynical people you'll ever meet.

MADYLN: The basic tool of our trade is attachment, which is another word for love. You can't get much less cynical than that.

STEPHANIE: But isn't it just a set-up? I mean, why should Alex attach to Kathy if he's just going to lose her anyway? Lose another mother? Why should I love Daniel if I'm just going to lose him?

ROSS: Because love is life and absence of love is death. Plain and simple.

STEPHANIE: Simple.

ROSS: But not easy.

STEPHANIE: It's so much work. And makes you so vulnerable. What are we asking these kids to do?

ROSS: I lived a lot of my life as unattached and isolated and stoned as possible.

STEPHANIE: That's hard to believe.

MADYLN: Believe it.

(During the following monologue ROSS circles the mannequin, pokes at it, pushes it over, sets it up again, squats in front of it, lies on the floor, sits beside it but not straight.)

ROSS: Debbie was my first love. We were sixteen. Our son was eleven days old. Andrew, after the father I never met, and we were on the streets. Living in a shelter, but we were trying to be a family. None of the three of us had a clue what family meant. Debbie and I were stoned all the time but the baby seemed okay, and it was raining, it had been raining his whole life, more than his whole life, rain for weeks, mud everywhere, the hills sliding down into the streets. I went out to get ice cream for Debbie, not to score dope or go to the liquor store or anything like that, I just meant to get her some strawberry ice cream with real strawberries in it like she liked, but first I had to get the money and I got distracted, made a couple of detours—

(MADLYN drapes a blanket over ROSS's head and shoulders.)

MADYLN: "A couple of detours," Ross?

ROSS: I ran into somebody in the park and we dropped acid and I was gone a long time, tripping out on the rain, the sound of the rain, the feel of it in my mouth. I was gone a long time. Days, maybe.

MADYLN: That's better. Can you do it by yourself now?

ROSS: Yes. Thank you. I love you.

MADYLN: I love you. *(MADLYN moves away.)*

ROSS: When I got back the shelter wasn't there. I thought I'd made a wrong turn. I was so high, all the time, I thought I got confused, or maybe Debbie and Drew were hallucinations or maybe acid gave me access to the reality they were in and if I got even more tripped out I'd find them again. It was raining. The hill was on top of the shelter, burying it, burying my family. People were digging. I tried to dig. The strawberry ice cream turned into mud.

MADYLN: He stayed there for a long time. Under the mud.

ROSS: It was safe there.

MADYLN: He thought it was safe there. It wasn't really.

ROSS: Buried alive.

MADYLN: Ears, eyes, nose, mouth, pores clogged with mud.

ROSS: Until somebody dug in and found me.

MADYLN: A counselor in a street-front program, who made him sit up straight and fight for his life.

(ROSS removes the blanket and joins the others.)

ROSS: I still fight. Every day. To take birth rather than death.

STEPHANIE: What an amazing story, Ross.

ROSS: The world is full of amazing stories. Redemption and transformation are there for the taking. But you have to take them.

STEPHANIE: Those are big words for a kid Alex's age.

MADYLN: You're right, Stephanie. We ask a lot.

STEPHANIE: You are so sure of yourselves! Don't you ever have doubts?

ROSS: Not about the work, but about ourselves, sure, all the time.

STEPHANIE: I'm exhausted. Is it okay if I go home?

MADYLN: Now's not the time—

ROSS: Sure, Stephanie, go home and rest and spend time with Daniel, do what you need to do to take care of yourself.

Stephanie *(to ROSS)*: Thank you. *(to MADLYN)* I'm sorry. *(STEPHANIE exits.)*

ROSS: Lighten up a little, MADLYN. This stuff is hard.

MADYLN: She's got potential. I hate to see her wimp out.

ROSS: Give her some time.

MADYLN: I'm worried about Alex. He's so dug in.

ROSS: Maybe this is one we can't save.

MADYLN: He's right on the verge. We have to be stronger than he is.

ROSS: We are. Together, we are.

(They kiss. As their embrace becomes passionate, lights down except spot on mannequin.)

SCENE TWENTY-FOUR

KATHY enters carrying a blanket. She swaddles the mannequin like a baby, only its head uncovered, and takes it onto her lap, rocking.

KATHY: You don't have to fight me, Alex. There's nothing to be scared of.

ALEX *(off-stage)*: Let go of me! I can't move!

KATHY: It's okay. Everything's all right.

ALEX *(off-stage)*: I can't breathe!

KATHY: We'll breathe together. Take slow, deep breaths. Come on, son, breathe with me.

ALEX *(off-stage)*: I can't breathe!

KATHY: Please, Alex, I need you to breathe with me.

ALEX *(off-stage)*: I can't breathe!

(KATHY shushes him and sings to him, rocking the mannequin.)

SCENE TWENTY-FIVE

Lights up on JASMINE, QUENTIN, BRODY, ROGER, and ALEX. Much strong movement from the adults (arguing, fighting, overtones of sex and violence) in which ALEX occasionally is included. QUENTIN and BRODY exit. ROGER exits, beckoning to JASMINE. JASMINE exits, reluctantly, looking back at her son. ALEX remains alone for a beat. Lights down except for the spot on KATHY and the mannequin.

SCENE TWENTY-SIX

KATHY: That's right, Alex, you can do it. Breathe! *(Beat. KATHY unwraps the mannequin, lays it down gently, kisses it, exits.)*

MADLYN (voice-over): Alexander Hahn! You sit up straight! Kathy, make him sit up straight.

KATHY *(off-stage)*: Oh, do I have to?

MADYLN: *(voice-over)*: Yes, you have to, if he's ever going to get well.

(KATHY enters, sits the mannequin up straight, exits. Pause with the mannequin straight-sitting in the spot. STEPHANIE enters, watches the mannequin from outside the spot.)

STEPHANIE: It wasn't really that they—that we believed we

were God. More that we were chosen, called, to do "the work." Arrogance, of course. Terrible, dangerous hubris. But if you have fire, wouldn't it also be hubris *not* to put it to use?

SCENE TWENTY-SEVEN

Lights up on KATHY, STEPHANIE, and MADLYN in the CAREYS' office.

MADYLN: —that's why you're here. You've paid us a lot of money and invested a lot of time and energy and hope in this process.

KATHY: But what if I'm wrong? What if you're wrong?

MADYLN: We're not wrong.

KATHY: How can you be so sure?

MADYLN: We couldn't do the work if we weren't sure.

KATHY: I'm not used to surrendering control like this. In my work I make the decisions.

MADYLN: That can help you do what you need to do here.

KATHY: You really think he needs to love me?

MADYLN: He needs to love somebody, some parent. And he already does love you. That's why he's fighting so hard.

KATHY: He's so scared.

MADYLN: We're all scared. Attachment is loving and being loved *even though* we're scared. Because we're scared.

KATHY: I think love feels dangerous for him.

MADYLN: Love is dangerous for all of us. Because it's so important.

KATHY: I need to love him, too.

MADYLN: I know.

KATHY: Is that all right?

MADYLN: It's essential.

KATHY: They say it shouldn't be about the parent's needs.

MADYLN: If the parent doesn't need the child, it might as well be an institution.

KATHY: They say not to take things personally.

MADYLN: This is the paradigm for all other personal relationships.

KATHY: I know you and Ross have adopted five children. I saw the pictures on your website.

MADYLN: Actually, I have adopted six. We got to raise only five.

KATHY: Oh, MADLYN, I'm sorry. I didn't know. How—how did it happen?

MADYLN: She didn't die. I gave her back. Crystal. My first child. Isn't that a pretty name?

KATHY: You adopted her and then gave her back to social services?

MADYLN: Yes.

KATHY: How could you— *(Beat.)* You said "My first child," not "Our."

MADYLN: I was a single mom. I knew I wanted children before I knew I wanted a husband. Ross doesn't know about Crystal.

KATHY: Oh. Why?

MADYLN: It's just—very—personal.

KATHY: You've been married twenty-five years.

MADYLN: Yes.

KATHY: Then why tell me? It's a lot—

MADYLN: I'm not sure. It feels right.

KATHY: What do you want me to—

MADYLN: Nothing. I don't want you to do anything.

KATHY: What happened? What'd she do? She must have been really difficult for you to—

MADYLN: It wasn't her. It was me. I promised to be her mother. That's a sacred word. And I betrayed her.

KATHY: How long did you have her?

MADYLN: Almost two years. But whether it had been a day or a decade, if she'd really been my child, if I'd really claimed her, it wouldn't have happened. If I'd been strong and brave and good enough.

KATHY: She must have been really tough.

MADYLN: Oh, she did all the stuff. The rages, the sexualized behavior, the crazy lying and fire-setting and animal cruelty, the self-mutilation, the preoccupation with her own excrement. But the thing I couldn't tolerate was her refusal to let me love her. She never stopped fighting. I couldn't live with feeling like a failure all the time.

KATHY: I get that.

MADYLN: She had serious attachment issues. And so did I. If I'd known then what I know now, I could have saved us both.

KATHY: I'm sure you did everything—

MADYLN: No. I didn't. I didn't keep her.

KATHY: I'm sorry, I didn't mean to—

MADYLN: Crystal was almost twelve when I gave her back to the system. She hadn't reached her growth yet. I don't know if she ever did. I don't know what her growth would have been. I gave up all my rights to wonder about that, but I still wonder.

(MADLYN wraps up in a blanket, covering herself completely including her head, leaving just enough of an opening that we can hear her. During the following monologue, ROSS enters, stands just onstage.)

Crystal. I say her name as often as I can, as penance. Crystal and I had had a good weekend together. We were both surprised. Nothing dramatic, just little mother-daughter things. We read aloud to each other. She was late learning to read, but by then she was good at it. I keep trying to remember what we read. She let me put her hair in a French braid, let me touch her all that time, thick long beautiful hair, she was finally keeping it clean, combing out the tangles herself so I didn't have to do it and maybe hurt her. We made dinner together. Spaghetti. We went for a walk.

There was a three-quarter moon. Details like that come into such sharp focus when it turns out to be the last time. Crystal held my hand. Tiny little thing but almost an adolescent, and she held my hand. About nine o'clock she said she was sleepy, and I tucked her in and kissed her good-night and sat up a while until I thought she was asleep and then I went to bed. And when I woke up the next morning my daughter was gone, along with fifty-four dollars and three credit cards from my purse and my new leather jacket. On the floor outside my bedroom door was a pile of her thick black hair.

(Pause. MADLYN unwraps the blanket, folds it, puts it away. She sees ROSS.)

And I gave up. I called the police and told them not to bring her home when they found her. I called the social worker and told him I was done. So Crystal was right all along. I didn't mean what I said about forever.

(*To ROSS*) Every day of my life is an atonement. Every child who breaks through is a dedication to Crystal.

(*To KATHY*) I disclose this to you, Kathy, because it's too late for my child. But it's not too late for yours.

(Lights down except spot on mannequin.)

SCENE TWENTY-EIGHT

Lights up on ROSS and MADLYN'S bedroom.

ROSS: Why didn't you tell me? I shouldn't have found out like this—

MADYLN: At first I was ashamed.

ROSS: I told you about the mud.

MADYLN: Then for a long time it was as if it had happened to somebody else, somebody who'd done a terrible thing but I could have compassion for her. Then as I learned about the work, I was afraid.

ROSS: Afraid of what? That it would hurt your reputation?

MADYLN: That it would get in the way. That I'd—that you'd think less of me.

ROSS: I wish you had—

MADYLN: That you'd leave me! (*Beat. Ross goes to her. They stand quietly together.*) I was afraid. (*Beat.*) I'm sorry.

ROSS: I love you.

(Lights down.)

SCENE TWENTY-NINE

Lights up on CAREYS' office. ROSS, MADLYN, and STEPHANIE speak in voice-over, ALEX and KATHY from offstage.

ROSS: If you aren't ready you don't have to do this, Stephanie. But once we're in there, you can't waver.

STEPHANIE: I'm ready.

MADYLN: Okay. Good. Kathy, are you there?

KATHY: I'm here.

ROSS: And you understand that we'll be saying and doing things that may seem harsh.

KATHY: Yes, I understand.

ROSS: And you don't intervene until you hear your cue.

KATHY: When one of you says, "Here he comes."

MADYLN: Then you get in there as fast as you can.

KATHY: I'm ready.

MADYLN: Okay, team, let's do it. Alexander Hahn, my love, you have met your match.

SCENE THIRTY

Therapy room. MADLYN, ROSS, and STEPHANIE enter, surround ALEX, wrap him tightly in the blanket. This should recall the dead puppy wrapped in the blanket.

ALEX: Let me go! Let me out of here!

MADYLN: You can get out if you want to, Alex. You have to want to really bad. That's what it takes.

(They cover his head and face with the blanket, wrapping it snugly.)

ALEX: I can't breathe!

STEPHANIE: Yes, you can. We'll make sure you have oxygen.

(They lay him on the floor. ROSS and MADLYN sit on him. STEPHANIE hesitates until she is wordlessly directed to sit, too.)

ALEX: Ow! You're heavy! Get off me, you're heavy!

MADYLN: Fight your way out, Alex. Come on, fight! Nobody's going to do it for you.

ROSS: It isn't easy being born, is it, Alex? Are you brave enough?

ALEX: You're too heavy! You're hurting me! You're squashing me!

MADYLN: Tell you what, Alex. When you're ready to be born, you just let us know, okay? We can wait. It's up to you.

ALEX: I can't breathe! You're squashing me! I'm dying!

(MADLYN and ROSS begin to chat.)

MADYLN: So, Ross, did you see that that wonderful house is for sale again? Our dream house?

ROSS: It's such a great place. All those windows and set in a mountain meadow like that. I bet it costs a fortune.

MADYLN: What's your dream house, Stephanie?

STEPHANIE: What?

ALEX: Please! I'm gonna die!

ROSS: If you could live in any house you wanted to—

MADYLN: —if you could build your own house any way you wanted—

ROSS: —create your own house—

MADYLN: —and if money and time were no object—

ROSS: —what would it be like?

STEPHANIE: I—I don't know.

ROSS: I'd have a glass ceiling in the bedroom so I could look at the stars.

MADYLN: And it would be self-cleaning, right? And heated to keep the snow off?

ROSS: And there'd be a way to keep birds from crashing into it.

MADYLN: And airplanes. And angels.

ALEX: Please, I can't breathe, you said you'd give me oxygen, you promised.

MADYLN: Come on, you little twerp, fight for your life.

ROSS: So, Stephanie, what kind of house would you build for yourself and your new husband if you could build it any way you wanted? No limits.

STEPHANIE: I don't know. It would be in the forest, I guess. He's choking.

MADYLN: What kind of forest? A pine forest? Redwoods?

STEPHANIE: What are we doing?

ROSS: We're waiting for Alex to decide to be born. It could take a while. We might as well amuse ourselves.

MADYLN: We don't want to work harder at it than he does.

STEPHANIE: It's hard to watch.

MADYLN: So is heart surgery.

ROSS: So would your house be big or small?

ALEX: You promised I could have oxygen!

STEPHANIE: Small. Cozy and small. No. No, it'd be huge, one huge open room. I don't know.

MADYLN: Tell us about your wedding. What are your colors?

STEPHANIE: Peach and mauve.

MADYLN: That's pretty. How many bridesmaids?

STEPHANIE: Four, and four groomsmen.

ROSS: I've never understood the concept of bridesmaids and groomsmen. What's their purpose?

STEPHANIE: They stand up with you.

MADYLN: They bear witness.

(For the first time, the mannequin's spot dims a little.)

SCENE THIRTY-ONE

Lights up on another part of the stage where JASMINE, carrying the mannequin, cavorts with the CHILDREN from the previous scenes. Once or twice JASMINE drops the mannequin. As the CHILDREN exit, JASMINE tries to catch them and calls out random names. Mannequin's spot up bright. Some time has passed.

SCENE THIRTY-TWO

Therapy Room.

STEPHANIE: —hope it doesn't rain.

MADYLN: That's the trouble with an outdoor wedding.

STEPHANIE: He peed himself.

ROSS: Enuresis and encopresis are common. Babies wet and soil themselves in the womb. It's okay. Kathy will clean him up later.

STEPHANIE: Hasn't he been quiet a long time?

MADYLN: Sometimes they are. We had an outdoor wedding, in the mountains.

ROSS: And it hailed.

MADYLN: It got caught in my veil. It was like looking out through stars—

(The conversation and the spot dim.)

SCENE THIRTY-THREE

Lights up on ROGER, QUENTIN, and BRODY silently but fiercely arguing. Roger gestures "get out" and pushes them toward the exits. After some resistance, they leave.

Lights down on ROGER. Again, some time has passed.

SCENE THIRTY-FOUR

Therapy room.

ALEX: I'm dying! I'm dying!
(Spot up full.)
ROSS: —Italian food, I think. There's a great place in our neighborhood.

STEPHANIE: Greek's my favorite. Or Ethiopian, maybe.

ROSS: Have we ever had Ethiopian, honey?

MADYLN: No. We should try it. I've never met food I didn't like.

STEPHANIE: Did he throw up?

MADYLN: A little nausea is to be expected.

ALEX: I threw up. It's all over me.

MADYLN: You can have a nice bath when you come out. Whenever you're ready.

ALEX: I'm not coming out.

ROSS: We're waiting for you, Alex. Your mom is waiting for you.

STEPHANIE: Life is waiting for you.

MADYLN: That's good, Stephanie. You might have a knack for this.

STEPHANIE: I have good teachers.

ALEX: I'm not coming out cuz I'm gonna die in here.

MADLYN *(smiles at the others)*: So die, then.

STEPHANIE: Wow.

MADYLN: It's a metaphor.

ALEX: Why do you want me to die? Does my mom want me to die, too?

KATHY: No!

ROSS: Sometimes dying is what it takes.

ALEX: Okay. I'm gonna die. I'm gonna die now. I'm sorry.

KATHY: Baby, don't you want to be reborn?

ALEX: No.

MADYLN: Hang on, everybody. We're getting close.

ROSS: He's really pushing it. Maybe we should—

MADYLN: Tonight I'm going to take a long bath. With bubbles. It's been kind of a stressful day.

STEPHANIE: Wish I could. I've got a test tomorrow.

ROSS: This is where I always have doubts.

MADYLN: We can't lose our nerve now, Ross.

ROSS: I won't. For his sake.

MADYLN: For all of us. For Crystal.

(Spot dims as lights come up suggesting fire. Pause. Lights down.)

ACT II

About a year after the end of Act I. In darkness, we hear a tape of the last scene of Act I which extends a few minutes beyond what was seen on stage.

ALEX: I'm not coming out cuz I'm gonna die in here.

MADYLN: So die, then.

STEPHANIE: Wow.

MADYLN: It's a metaphor.

ALEX: Why do you want me to die? Does my mom want me to die, too?

KATHY: No!

ROSS: Sometimes dying is what it takes.

ALEX: Okay. I'm gonna die. I'm gonna die now. I'm sorry.

KATHY: Baby, don't you want to be reborn?

ALEX: No.

MADYLN: Hang on, everybody. We're getting close.

ROSS: He's really pushing it. Maybe we should—

MADYLN: Tonight I'm going to take a long bath. With bubbles. It's been kind of a stressful day.

STEPHANIE: Wish I could. I've got a test tomorrow.

ROSS: This is where I always have doubts.

MADYLN: We can't lose our nerve now, Ross.

ROSS: I won't. For his sake.

MADYLN: For all of us. For Crystal.

(Tape continues with a scene we haven't seen before.)

STEPHANIE: Hasn't he been quiet for a long time?

MADYLN: Sometimes it takes—

ROSS: No! Something's wrong!

MADYLN: Ross, don't—

STEPHANIE: Oh, my God!

(Lights up on courthouse hallway. SAM approaches JASMINE.)

SAM: Jasmine—

JASMINE: How do you know my name? Did my son tell you my name? *(Beat.)*

SAM: Yes. Alex told me.

JASMINE: Who are you?

SAM: I'm—*(SAM's voice breaks.)* I'm his grandpa.

JASMINE: I'm his mother!

SAM *(indicates the trash bag)*: What's in the bag?

JASMINE: All I got left.

SAM: My daughter can't look at anything of his.

JASMINE: Me, I want it by me.

SAM: It's too hard on her. I had to pack everything away.

JASMINE: That'd be like losing him all over again.

SAM: Yeah, I kept a few things out.

JASMINE: Did he love you?

SAM: I think so. Anyway, we were buddies.

JASMINE: See? They keep saying all that about "attachment." He didn't have to love you, you weren't even his real granddad, you know? But he did. That's my boy. Maybe not the best-behaved child in the world, but he did know how to love.

SAM: I loved him, too. *(Beat.)*

JASMINE: So I heard your daughter got probation.

SAM: And community service.

JASMINE: What a bunch of crap.

SAM: She loved him, too, you know.

JASMINE: Could've fooled me, what she let them do to him.

SAM: She was trying to get him help.

JASMINE: What'd he need help for? He was just a little boy.

SAM: He had problems.

JASMINE: We all got problems. Lord knows I do. Don't you?

SAM: Yeah. I have problems.

JASMINE: Doesn't your daughter have problems?

SAM: Yeah, sure, but—

JASMINE: We all got problems. Like what kind of problems are you saying Alex had?

SAM: He threw temper tantrums like I've never seen before. For hours at a time.

JASMINE: Well, maybe he was mad because he wasn't with his mama. You ever think of that?

SAM: He was with his mother. He had two mothers.

JASMINE: You get one mama and one daddy in this life. That's all you get.

(JASMINE sways, grabs SAM's arm to steady herself.)

SAM: You all right?

JASMINE: I gotta sit down. It's hot in here. Why's it so hot in here? (JASMINE sits.)

SAM: Do you need—can I get you anything?

JASMINE: It's a boy. You carry boys higher. His name's Alexander.

SAM: You can't do that.

JASMINE: Course I can. That's one thing I can do, name my baby what I want. His name's Alex. Alexa if it's a girl. But it's not.

SAM: You got anybody to help you? Where's that guy? (SAM looks around for ROGER.)

JASMINE: My mama'll come and help me. When it's time. But it's not time yet. How come Kathy didn't just have her own?

SAM: Alex was her own.

JASMINE: Instead of stealing somebody else's?

SAM: Oh, come on. He was available for adoption. Court took away your rights because of—

JASMINE: Is she barren or what?

SAM: She never married.

JASMINE: Yeah? So?

SAM: She could have had kids the usual way, far as I know. She wanted to adopt.

JASMINE: Why would anybody do that? It's not natural.

SAM: She said she wanted to be a mother and there were already kids out there who needed parents.

JASMINE: Like Alex.

SAM: Yeah, like Alex.

JASMINE: Alex had a mama.

SAM: You couldn't take care of him. You didn't take care of him.

JASMINE: How would *you* know? I took care of him just fine.

SAM: They took him away from you.

JASMINE: They had no right.

SAM: Kathy was told he was abused and neglected. Social services has the records.

JASMINE: It's a lie.

SAM: They said he was beaten up more than once.

JASMINE: Brody's got a temper, that's true, but I protected my son best I could, took it myself so he wouldn't get after him. That's what mothers do, protect their kids.

SAM: They said he was most likely—molested.

JASMINE: What?

SAM: Sexually. *(Beat.)* Look, I didn't come here to—

JASMINE: He swore to me he didn't do that.

SAM: Who? This Brody character? He better be behind bars.

JASMINE: Not him. Somebody else.

SAM: That joker who was here with you? Where is he?

JASMINE: Somebody else. He swore to me. If I knew he did that to my baby—

SAM: He was a fire-setter.

JASMINE: A lot of little kids play with matches. Especially boys. I don't know why that is.

SAM: It was more than that. They said it was because of the abuse.

JASMINE: Did you come here just to tell me how evil my son was?

SAM: He wasn't evil. He was a great kid. But he was—messed

up. Troubled. That's what I'm trying to tell you. So you'll know
why—

JASMINE: My son wasn't sick! Don't you say that about
him!

SAM: He smeared his poop on the walls. He would eat until
he threw up because he couldn't tell when he was full. He—

JASMINE: Don't talk like that about the dead!

SAM: He killed a puppy.

JASMINE: Oh, poor baby, he loved animals, he must've been
so sad—

SAM: He was.

JASMINE: He always was soft-hearted.

SAM: Yeah, he was. He named the puppy Ja— *(Beat.)* I loved
him. *(Beat.)* I didn't think I would. I thought Kathy was crazy. I
didn't think you could ever really feel like somebody else's kid
was yours. *(Beat.)* At first when we went camping, he'd wake up
screaming, somebody was going to kill him, or he was by him-
self in the woods, even if I was right there. That's one reason I
got him the puppy. He named him Jazz. Jazz was the first thing
I saw him really let go and love.

JASMINE: I was his mama. He had to love me. His first
mama.

SAM: I didn't want her to adopt, especially not an older kid
with problems. I was a cop for a lot of years. I saw how those
kids turn out.

JASMINE: You were a cop?

SAM: I sure as hell didn't want to love him.

JASMINE: What d'you want from me?

SAM: I want to know who Alex was before he was my
grandson.

JASMINE: Why? So you can tell the judge it was my fault he
died?

SAM: No—

JASMINE: So you can say I'm an unfit mother and they'll
take this baby, too?

SAM: Stop it.

JASMINE: So your daughter can steal this baby from me,
too? Do it right this time?

CHORUS MEMBER 2: I'll take him.

CHORUS MEMBER 1: I'll take him.

CHORUS MEMBERS 3 and 4: We'll take him.

CHORUS CHILD 2: You can come home with us.

(KATHY and STEPHANIE enter along with other courtroom observers.)

SAM: *Shut up now.* There's the jury.

(Lights up on a set suggesting a courtroom where two cardboard cut-outs, which will now represent ROSS and MADLYN until the last scene, are straight-sitting. Out of a trash bag JASMINE begins taking items she associates with ALEX and arranging them on the floor and on the bench between her and ROGER. STEPHANIE is surrounded by CHORUS MEMBERS.)

CHORUS MEMBER 1: Alex never had a chance from the moment he was born till the moment he died.

CHORUS MEMBER 2: His mother, Jasmine Simmons, meant for him to have the chance she never had.

CHORUS MEMBER 3: Giving a kid a chance doesn't seem to be something his father thought much about. Whoever his father was.

CHORUS MEMBER 4: The social workers did everything they could to give these kids a chance.

STEPHANIE: Kathy and Sam Hahn, his mother and grandfather, tried to give him every opportunity in life. That's what brought them to us. I came to believe with MADLYN and Ross Carey that we were his last chance.

CHORUS MEMBER 2: What kind of parent would subject her child to something like that?

CHORUS MEMBER 4: Desperate. Afraid.

CHORUS CHILD 1: Mean! She was mean!

CHORUS MEMBER 1: The risks were just too great.

CHORUS MEMBER 3: But so were the possible benefits.

CHORUS MEMBER 1: Bottom line, they killed him. And his adoptive mom let it happen.

CHORUS CHILD 2: Meanie!

JASMINE: This was his favorite toy when he was a baby.

ROGER: Well, sure, his old man give it to him. Got it at the dollar store over town.

JASMINE: Santa gave it to him his first Christmas. That church Santa.

ROGER *(indicating a photo)*: I got this one in my wallet to show people. Took it myself. You nursing him.

JASMINE: You never would hold him.

ROGER: Seemed like he'd break. Now I wish I did.

JASMINE: I guess he did break. I guess they broke him.

ROGER: Guess anybody can break, enough happens to them.

JASMINE *(taking a lock of hair out of a baggie)*: Oh, look!

ROGER: What is that?!

JASMINE: From his first haircut.

ROGER: He never had hair that color.

JASMINE: Sure, he did, when he was little. You just forgot.

ROGER: He never in his life had hair that color.

(JASMINE touches ROGER's cheek with the lock of hair.)

JASMINE: Feel how soft.

ROGER: Get that away from me!

JASMINE: See how it curls around your finger.

ROGER: Like some kind of damn voodoo!

(JASMINE puts the lock of hair back into the baggie and sets it carefully on the bench, then digs in the trash bag again.)

JASMINE *(holding up a onesie)*: How cute! Can you believe he was so little? I'm gonna save this for the new baby.

ROGER: Got some dirty diapers in there you're gonna save, too?

JASMINE: Oh, I almost forgot about his ducky. One time he threw it out of the tub and I had to go crawling around on the floor to find it and he kind of slipped down in the water and he started choking. Scared me to death. Spanked his little bottom and told him to never ever do that to his mama again, and he never did. He was such a good little baby. Oh, and here's his favorite truck from when he was maybe two.

ROGER: Give me that. This ain't his. This was mine when I was little.

JASMINE: You sure it wasn't his? I thought it was his.

ROGER: How'd you come to have it there in that old garbage bag?

JASMINE: Maybe you gave it to him? Sometimes daddies

give their stuff to their kids—

ROGER: You and your kid better leave my shit alone, you hear me?

JASMINE *(takes out an adult-size cap)*: This you did give him, remember?

ROGER: I guess.

JASMINE: His third birthday, remember, babe? He was in that foster home?

ROGER: Yeah. I guess. *(JASMINE holds up a frilly baby dress and oooh's over it.)* That ain't his for sure!

JASMINE: Doesn't matter. Makes me think of babies.

ROGER: You never put him in that, did you? No son of mine—

JASMINE: Course not. It's pretty, though, don't you think?

ROGER: But what's it doing in there? It wasn't his. *(JASMINE takes out part of a cardboard box, pieces of Styrofoam, a paper towel tube.)* That's just trash.

JASMINE: Yeah, but he played with it. He could've played with it. Times when we didn't have toys. Even when we did.

(ROGER reaches into the bag.)

ROGER: Bullets? What the hell?

JASMINE: Don't you think they're kind of cute? Kind of like little toys?

ROGER: You are one crazy lady, you know that?

JASMINE: When I was pregnant with Alex I used to read to him and play that classical music because I heard it would make my baby smart. Did, too.

ROGER: Lotta brains in my family. My mom's always got her nose in some book. She likes those romance things.

JASMINE: I don't even like that kind of music, but it was for my baby. I do it for this one, too.

ROGER *(sincerely)*: You're a good mama, Jasmine.

JASMINE: Am I?

ROGER: The best. *(He puts his arm around her.)*

JASMINE: My mama left me on a street corner when I was four years old and I had to dig in garbage cans.

ROGER: I know, baby. You been telling me that ever since I knew you.

CHORUS MEMBER 1: Skinny, dirty little thing.

CHORUS MEMBER 2: Timid little thing, scared of her own shadow.

CHORUS CHILD 3: Don't be scared.

CHORUS MEMBER 3: What do you expect, a child treated like that.

CHORUS MEMBER 1: Sweet, though. Those big eyes, and those curls.

CHORUS MEMBER 4: One time I found Alex walking along the road looking for his mama. Couldn't have been more than two years old.

JASMINE: Yes, he was. He was twenty-six months. I had to take Mama to work and Alex was sick and I didn't want to bother him and we couldn't have Mama lose her job—

ROGER: Should've called me.

JASMINE: I did. You weren't there.

CHORUS MEMBER 3: Whatever, that little boy was left home alone.

JASMINE: It was just for a few minutes. What else was I supposed to do?

CHORUS MEMBER 3: He was out looking for his mama.

CHORUS CHILD 4: Mama!

CHORUS CHILD 5: Where's your mama?

CHORUS MEMBER 3: I called the cops.

JASMINE: And that's what started the whole thing.

CHORUS MEMBER 3: What else was I supposed to do?

ROGER: Should've called me.

JASMINE: Whenever they took me away from my mama, I found a way to get back, so I always held out hope Alex'd find a way back to me.

ROGER: He would have, too. If he had the time.

JASMINE: I told those social workers, if you take him away from me it'll kill him. And that's exactly what they did.

STEPHANIE: Everybody has a version of Alex's story.

CHORUS MEMBER 2: Jasmine's mama was a foster kid, too. I know her since she's been born. Goes back a long ways.

CHORUS MEMBER 4: Alex had a recurring nightmare that he was being murdered.

CHORUS MEMBER 1: He told the social worker, "Maybe

when I was a very little boy my mama pushed me out a high-up window and I fell on my head and that's why I'm bad."

JASMINE: That's not true! One time he was running and he fell down a couple of steps—

CHORUS MEMBER 4: Right after he came to Kathy's he told a new little friend, "You're lucky. Your mama wants you."

JASMINE: That's a lie! He never said that!

CHORUS MEMBER 2: He said, "Kathy's my new mama. She wants me."

CHORUS CHILD 1: Your mama wanted you.

JASMINE: You only get one mama. I'm it. What I did was God's will. What they did was they played god with my child.

CHORUS MEMBER 1: Jasmine and her mama both had 100% desire to be good mothers. Trouble is, they were never taught how.

CHORUS MEMBER 3: It would be like me wanting to go to a hospital and save somebody's life. You'd have to show me how, wouldn't you?

CHORUS MEMBER 2: He was physically and sexually abused. He was exposed to domestic violence. How could she just not know any better?

CHORUS MEMBER 1: And anyway it's not about her. It's about the child.

CHORUS MEMBER 2: It wasn't a perfect situation, I'll give you that. But to my knowledge he was always fed, always clothed, always housed.

CHORUS MEMBER 1: Always loved.

STEPHANIE: Love. Now there's a word. In order to live a human life we have to act as if we know what it means.

CHORUS MEMBER 4: I bet social services'll take this one right from the hospital.

JASMINE: It's my baby! I'm the mama!

ROGER: Quiet now.

JASMINE: I'm gonna do it right with this one. You watch.

ROGER: Shut up!

(CHORUS MEMBERS *take their seats as courtroom observers.* SAM *and* KATHY *enter.*)

KATHY: I didn't expect the press. I guess I should have.

SAM: It's a big story. It's got good and evil, and people think they know which is which.

KATHY: Look at all these people.

SAM: Still want to stay?

KATHY: I have to be here.

SAM: The judge didn't say you had to do this.

KATHY: No, Dad, it's not part of my probation. I just have to be here.

ROGER *(to JASMINE)*: You better put that shit away or they'll confiscate it.

CHORUS MEMBER 4: Alexander Simmons Hahn was tortured.

STEPHANIE: For the purpose of healing. Like heart surgery, or chemotherapy.

CHORUS MEMBER 2: He was grabbed by the face.

CHORUS MEMBER 3: Screamed at.

CHORUS CHILD 3: Don't do that!

CHORUS MEMBER 1: Forced to sit straight and unmoving for long periods of time.

STEPHANIE: It was aggressive, last-chance treatment for a life-threatening illness.

CHORUS MEMBER 4: Forced to lie in his own bodily fluids.

CHORUS CHILD 4: I'm telling!

STEPHANIE: Would it have been better if we had this tool and didn't use it to try to help him?

CHORUS MEMBER 2: It was cruelty of a depraved and sickening nature.

STEPHANIE: Maybe it would have been better. I don't know.

CHORUS MEMBER 3: He was deprived of air.

STEPHANIE: I promised him he'd have oxygen. I thought that was a given.

JASMINE: Why would they do that to my baby?

CHORUS MEMBER 1 *(adjust numbers according to weights of actors)*: Three adults, a total of almost five hundred pounds, sat on this ninety-pound child.

CHORUS MEMBER 2: They wrapped him in a blanket and covered his face.

CHORUS MEMBER 4: On the tape you can hear him

screaming that he can't breathe. Nobody paid any attention.

JASMINE: Pay attention! You're supposed to pay attention to kids!

STEPHANIE: We were. Kathy couldn't think of anything else. MADLYN and Ross talked about him all the time. For me the entire universe had focused down to this one little boy.

CHORUS MEMBER 1: They were chatting among themselves about trivial things while this child fought for his life.

STEPHANIE: We couldn't do it for him. It wouldn't work if we wanted it more than he did.

ROGER: We don't need this.

STEPHANIE: Life was waiting for him, if he would choose it.

CHORUS MEMBER 1: They let him die.

(The following conversations between KATHY and SAM and between ROGER and JASMINE take place simultaneously.)

SAM: Are you okay? Should we leave?

ROGER: Let's get out of here.

KATHY and JASMINE *(not quite in sync)*: No. I owe it to Alex to be here.

SAM: We can leave.

KATHY: You wanted to come.

SAM: I can take you home and come back.

ROGER: Come on, babe, let's go home.

KATHY: Why do you want to be here, anyway?

SAM: He was my grandson.

JASMINE: He was my baby.

KATHY: I know. I'm sorry.

JASMINE: The least I can do is find out what he went through.

SAM: I've got to understand what happened.

KATHY: I know.

SAM: But I can take you home—

KATHY: No!

ROGER: I don't need this.

JASMINE: Suit yourself. I'm staying put.

ROGER: I'm not leaving you here.

JASMINE: I can take care of myself.

ROGER: We're in this together.

SAM: You've got to control yourself, then.

KATHY: Am I embarrassing you, Dad? Sorry.

SAM: They'll throw us out.

KATHY: I think that's his birthmother. She has his picture.
(KATHY stands.)

SAM: Where you going?

KATHY: To introduce myself.

SAM: Don't make a scene.

CHORUS MEMBER 2: It took a lot of nerve to videotape what they were doing to him.

STEPHANIE: All rebirthing sessions were taped, for training purposes. The Careys prided themselves on being their own toughest critics.

CHORUS MEMBER 2: You'd think they'd have destroyed it before the ambulance got there.

STEPHANIE: We weren't trying to hide anything.

CHORUS MEMBER 2: They came to believe they were God's gift to hurt children.

STEPHANIE: Yes.

CHORUS MEMBER 4: Pioneers. Visionaries.

STEPHANIE: Yes.

CHORUS MEMBER 1: Saviors.

STEPHANIE: It was transformation, not just treatment. Of the children and of ourselves. "This work is metamorphosis. It will change you and it will change the world." That's heady stuff.

CHORUS MEMBER 3: They did help a lot of very troubled children and desperate families.

STEPHANIE: And you could feel their passion. For the work and for each other. I wanted passion.

CHORUS MEMBER 2: The sessions with Alex weren't out of the ordinary for the kind of work they were doing.

CHORUS MEMBER 4: Except that he fought harder and longer.

STEPHANIE: It was scary, and exciting. We were working right on the edge. Ross and MADLYN said we had to be stronger than he was. I'd never been called upon to be strong.

CHORUS MEMBER 1: It's not uncommon for these children to say they can't breathe or they're hungry or they have to go to the bathroom or their arm hurts. Therapists call it somatic resistance.

CHORUS CHILD 5: I gotta go!

CHORUS MEMBER 4: It's not uncommon for them to struggle and scream. Being born is scary.

CHORUS MEMBER 3: We ask a lot of our children. It's hard work.

CHORUS MEMBER 4: You have to be brave.

STEPHANIE: I'd never had to be brave before in my life.

CHORUS MEMBER 4: You have to be brave to live a truly human life.

KATHY: No shit.

JASMINE: I'm scared all the time.

SAM: Shh!

STEPHANIE: Ross and MADLYN Carey felt called to help children everybody else had given up on. I wanted to be called, too.

(Ignoring SAM's attempts to stop her, KATHY sits beside JASMINE. JASMINE moves as far away from KATHY as she can on the bench and puts the trash bag between them. KATHY begins taking objects out of the trash bag and putting them in her lap. JASMINE tries to pull the bag away, but KATHY holds on. An object falls noisily.)

This is the most important thing that's ever happened to me. Maybe the only important thing. I was there. I should have stopped it. But when, exactly? How close do you come to the edge?

(KATHY and JASMINE are both crying.)

CHORUS MEMBER 4: The Careys are icons in the attachment community. They have many devoted supporters.

CHORUS MEMBER 3: They gave my child back to me.

CHORUS MEMBER 2: It was the miracle our family prayed for.

CHORUS MEMBER 1: My son had been seriously trying to take his own life since he was six years old. Medications, hospitalization, all kinds of therapy—nothing made any difference until we found ross and MADLYN. He owes his life to them.

CHORUS MEMBER 3: Because of them, our daughter can live in the world instead of in a mental institution or prison. She owes her freedom to them.

CHORUS MEMBER 4: The only hope for a severely attachment-disordered child like Alex is if someone, somehow can break through.

CHORUS MEMBER 1: Break in.

CHORUS CHILD 1: Thanks.

(ROSS and MADLYN enter with blankets like the one used to wrap ALEX in Act I. They wrap the mannequins as if for rebirthing, carry them offstage, return and straight-sit where the mannequins were.)

MADYLN: I have come to regard the story of Alexander Hahn, his life and his death, as the quintessential great American tragedy.

JASMINE: That's not true! He had joy!

SAM: He had fun.

ROSS: We meant to be healers. Instead we destroyed him. I will never forgive myself.

MADYLN: Coming into contact with this terrible event, becoming part of it in such an intimate way, has plunged me into a dark night of the soul.

ROSS: We believed in the possibility of transformation.

MADYLN: We still do.

ROSS: We believed ourselves to be agents of that transformation when no one else could be.

MADYLN: We still do. More than ever now, we must believe in the power and possibility of transformation.

ROSS: We are personally responsible for his tragic death.

MADYLN: If we'd held back, we'd have been personally responsible for his tragic life.

ROSS: I am so sorry. We should have been more careful. If I'd only checked on him a few minutes earlier—

MADYLN: I will mourn Alex Hahn for the rest of my life. But I have no regrets about doing everything I knew to do for him.

ROSS: I am guilty. I accept the jury's verdict and the court's judgment. I will never be able to atone for what I've done.

MADYLN: I have done everything I could do. The rest is up to someone else. I am very sad, but I am at peace.

(CHORUS MEMBERS and CHILDREN move around the stage in dance-like movements reminiscent of the earlier dance scenes, speaking over each other.)

CHORUS MEMBER 2: —a glass ceiling for looking at the stars, with a way to keep airplanes and birds and angels from crashing into it—

CHORUS MEMBER 1: —it had been raining his whole life, more than his whole life—

CHORUS MEMBER 3: —she hadn't reached her growth yet—

CHORUS CHILD 3: —okay, I give up, ollyollyinfree—

CHORUS MEMBER 2: Alex! Come in now, it's getting dark. Alex?

CHORUS MEMBER 4: —rain for weeks, mud everywhere, the hills sliding down into the streets—

STEPHANIE: I think every version of this story is true—

CHORUS MEMBER 4: —every day is an atonement—

CHORUS MEMBER 2: —every child who breaks through is a dedication—

STEPHANIE: —and every version of this story is false—

CHORUS MEMBER 3: —takes courage to live a life—

STEPHANIE: Including this one.

JASMINE *(to audience)*: Please, someone, won't you take my baby?

KATHY: Oh, Alex!

(Lights down.)

ROSS: Something's wrong!

MADYLN: Oh, my God!

ALEX: Mama?

END OF PLAY

POEMS

The Walk

Rounding a bend I barely
see, in a road I
barely see,
perceive—imperfectly, suggestively—
in the soles, balls, arches of my feet.
Rounding a bend
that announces itself to me only
by a shift in perspective
in this long rain.
I'm startled by
thick, contained, white, pulsing—
What is it? It takes me a moment to realize—
fog.
It fills more than half the field
of my vision.
It churns. I feel it
churning
though none of it touches me.
(How does one know, with fog?)
Lost
I may be
unable to find my way. Certainly disoriented,
(it happens as often as not),
and what would I do? Oh,
what will I do?
I may be simply seeing wrong.
It happens.

It's the lake. It's where the lake is. Now
I can catch my breath.
The sweet little valley brims with
fog.
And I stop to take it
in, transformed
as always, in one way or another,
subtly as fog,
profoundly as this bowled white fog,
the way I
see.

Primordial Haiku

Hypnagogic kiss:
Scales against my labia,
Toothmarks on your flank.
Sex in the daylight.
But I remember pincers
And a carapace.
"We are," she told me,
"Predator and prey." Into
My mouth, her tongue forked.
Clitoris and beak,
Public plumes and scrotal nest:
Child with hollow bones.
Pincers. Cloven tongue.
A hollow bone.
Inside me,
Deeper and deeper.

The Whole Field No One Sees

(for Mary Lou)

I hadn't heard this story.
Best friends for nearly forty
years, and you still make me
catch my breath:
The painting teacher took you
to the window. "Look." You
remember knowing vaguely
what he meant
before he asked, "What colors
do you see?"
"Brown," you muttered.
"Green." Was the tree an oak?
I will guess.
He waited. "Red," you told him.
"Purple. Yellow, orange, in
the creases of the bark."
He said
yes.
That moment set your vision.
In my imagination
his excitement pleases me,
and your pride,

and my need to re-consider
this man—hardly remembered
and dismissed too easily—
in new light.
My own inability
when I look at an oak tree
to see beyond the browns
pleases, too.
I don't need to see yellow
or to look out that window
to find what the teacher found
if you do.
What's beautiful and what's real
are layered, and the whole field
no one sees. So talk to me
about red
in tree trunks. About purple
in grass. About the circle
in the zigzag of a leaf.
About friends.

Samhain

I saw my ghost just now.
She saw me, too, knew me first,
waiting to make herself
known. I hadn't expected her yet.
We never do, not
yet. She looks just like me. I was shocked.
We always are.
Bonfires snaggled the hilltop
like pumpkin teeth
at sunset, reflecting both ways
through the veil so
thin tonight between our worlds
there might be none at all,
though we know there is.
Purified and, even
so, protected from each other,
needing protection,
we passed to drum and chant
between two lesser
fires. "Dance with me." I will
die within the year.
Here's what to do:
Celebrate me. It's about time.
Honor me with an empty place at table.
Eat for me as many as you can stand
of my sister's dry white cookies
she insists are cakes
for the dead. I'll be keeping score,
trying as always,
to gauge what I owe you.

I never thought I'd say this, but
I'll miss those cakes. I'll miss your father's
good amber ale. I'll miss
the moonlight firelight sunlight moon again
across your mouth. I'll miss—
or maybe not.
This means next time you'll have to leave
a westward window open
for me, and you'll have to
invite me
home for this party and even then
I'm sorry but I might not come.

Poem Cycle For Esther:

Things We Both Know

1. Adoption

We give them not birth, but
welcome.
We bring them not into
this world, but
for a short while,
through it.
We have no choice but to
know
what every parent ought to:
the miracle of
ours/not ours.
We are both real and not
real.
In this world,
another name for miracle is
chaos,
another:
the natural order of things.
This miracle,
our children,
belongs to us, and
not.

Uncommon Name

A weed thrives
in the front yard
along the north fence,
behind the pocked beds where
last autumn squirrels
paced
as I buried tulip bulbs at their feet
and dug up most of them
for winter hoarding
right through the chicken wire
before I was even indoors,
not far from the tub of petunias
allegedly foolproof
that dried up during a July heat wave
no one else's garden
noticed.
A weed because I
neither planned nor planted nor otherwise
willed it there.
Declares the gardener, who doesn't much like
me
but has pledged to take care of my site:
"Cancer of the garden
is its common name.
Because it's invasive."

(This is the same man,
gay-gangsta hat and
haughty hands, who said
the vigorous spiny volunteer
looping under and up through my juniper hedge,
six inches from one summer morning to the next,
roots utterly unassailable,
is called
matrimony vine

because it's prickly,
and I said it's
because it can withstand anything,
and we both glared
thinly, noting our hostilities.
But cancer
of the garden
is quite another matter.
He's gone past not amused to
grim.)
Not exactly protesting
or meaning to be revisionist,
not
looking at him out of
something like shyness,
I say, "But it has these graceful purple flowers,
and if you get close enough,
a slight sweet fragrance."
He shades his narrow eyes.
Do you think we can come to regard
cancer
not as the body turning on itself,
but as the body transforming?

2. Mastectomy

(which means
your breasts get cut off;
which means no
nipples)
not as mutilation but as
a different form of
beauty?
And pain
as pain, but also
as joy?
And fear as
awe?

If we can,
would that be cheating somehow?
Or growing?
Evading the truth, or
expanding it?
Someday, may I
touch your scars?

3. The Car

That last summer,
my father would say a car was waiting in the woods for
him, covered by underbrush, camouflaged by trees.
Can't you just see it? A humped shape that could be
anything, but isn't?
He'd see the car
if seeing is what it was
all of a sudden, and his slipping gaze would
light on it,
light up.
But maybe by then his fear
had come to feel to me like curiosity
and I didn't understand he was
afraid.
That last fall,
my father used to say he had one foot in another
world already. And smile.
But maybe by then the rage he'd promised
had disguised itself
for me as serenity,
and I didn't understand he was angry.
My father came not to know my name
but still that I was his daughter.
Then
not to know I was his child
or that he'd had a child
but still that I was someone important.
Then

not to know I was there at all
but still
for the first time since he was seven and
his mother died and
they said don't cry you're a man don't cry,
and he didn't,
to speak—
to repeat, because he'd forget
he'd just said it, and
every time it gave
him such new pleasure—
love.

4. Turning Fifty

I didn't know when you turned fifty
Because you called it something else,
Forty-three, perhaps, or
Purple,
Which we shall wear when we're old women, but
I say:
Why wait?

Dinner Conversations

(for David)

The waitress came with herbal tea and more plum wine
as you and I were talking about death, mine
particularly, since I'd been obsessed of late.
She didn't bat an eye or even hesitate,
just set about describing daily specials, took
our order, brought our food without a second look.
She was a pretty girl. I liked the way her arms
moved in and out of lamplight. No sign of alarm
or even interest when words like "cancer," "God,"
"epiphany" rolled off our tongues. I thought I could
imagine her report back in the kitchen, as
she waited for our curried shrimp and lemon grass.

It makes me smile to think how many hours we've spent
at red-checked tables, bars, buffets, booths with sprung   seats,
talking and listening. It's really all we do.
Lovers at first, we used to talk about that, too,
to the bemusement of our friends: How free we were,
how fortunate, how wild our passion was, how pure.
We must have been insufferable. We had no
shame, and deserved none. We're just as shameless now.
We publicly discuss things far more intimate
than sex. Our conversations are as passionate
as anything we've ever done together.
In matters of discourse, you are still my lover.

Silent Letter

"Jon."
Thinking your name without the h
because that's how I'd known you,
never mind all those letters,
silent, really,
announcing you had no need now for the youthful affectation,
no time now.
Ashamed, as though you'd know,
as though the presumptuous silent letter came
between us, set up false
inchoate rhyme and rhythm,
or offered a bridge neither of us could travel
through chaos.
Rheumy gray eyes in deep gray chasms,
tongue coated with grief's thrush for
your lover, your music,
Hands on the table bright flickering translucent as
ghosts. Sepulchral
body and shadow of body aghast
at the world it must still make its way through.
"Jon? Are you sick?"
"No!" you
sighed.

The Day I Rode Go-carts With My Son

(for Chris)

You told me I should drive
and I agreed.
Your father pointed out
I'm nearly blind,
then went away to watch.
This was between us. But
at the first curve
you had to take the wheel,
the angle wrong,
reach awkward from your side.
I could still shift the gears
and give it gas.
I might have lost my nerve,
let go, without
your silent half-smile dare.
My hand was on the clutch,
my foot down hard.
We took the turns too fast.
I knew we would.
That's why I rode with you.
We swerved from lane to lane,
tailgated, cut

the other drivers off.
My graying hair,
your prison-made tattoo,
my lust to know what's real,
your contraband—
I could have touched the wall
hot hurtling past.

I could have cried again
for you. But this was good
for me, this speed,
this danger sharp and small,
this outlaw ride
that wouldn't last for long.
Much has come between us
in nineteen years.
Sometimes when I despair—
secrets you hoard,
how far apart we live—
I think of go-carts, and
It is enough.

Taking Nourishment

(for Veronica)

Somebody wise, and in a position to know,
said to me once of you,
"With everything she's been through, it's a wonder"—
speaking to me of you—"a wonder
she can even sit up and take nourishment."
I was stunned.
This sorrow, though not new,
had now been gathered.
My poor little girl.
But
In your green plaid dress with the white collar
up a long sunny sidewalk hill
you came running
"mommymommymommy"
into my arms.
While the man was hurting you
and calling it love,
you knew to curl in your daddy's lap
and call it what it was:
love.
When your brother died
and I thought the world had ended
or ought to,
you leaned outside your own grief
into your father's and mine,
which must have been a scary place,
and took our faces in your small hands.

And yesterday,
terrified, offering you
my hurt places,
I was in the presence of

a woman.
You do
take nourishment,
and you nourish me.
Sorrow's only the half of it.
The other half's the
wonder.

Sonnet For A Writer Friend

(for Ed)

The story was a good one, not your best,
I think, but with a certain crisp elan.
"I don't mind pain," your character confessed.
"I wouldn't say that to just any man."
You hadn't asked permission. Did I care?
And, anyway, who owns the spoken word?
My first reaction was that you had dared
To make our playful passion seem absurd.
But now I've come to treasure tangled things—
A skein of jazz; a variegated riff
Of family; the chaos prayer brings;
The way a friendship braids into a life;
The curse and blessing of a writer. And
I wouldn't say that to just any man.

Two Stories From My Son

(for Joe)

You bring me stories out of your life
like yo-yos, joyous
jumping
little discs on a string.
Two today, crisscrossing
in midair:
how you saved a bird's life on your way to kung fu, and
how you're getting rich in Spanish class.
The bird was stuck,
one foot and the rest of it
on either side of a wooden fence.
With delicate fingers and thumbs you show me
how you spread the boards
to free its leg,
pausing in the telling to marvel,
"So small."
The teacher rewards new words, new
concepts, and the willingness to
declare them
with photocopied pesos.
Four hundred in your wrinkled envelope already;
smug, you tell me, "some kids don't even have ten.
They're the poor people."

I can see you:
lurking
in position
so you can be in the right place at the right time
to *cierra la puerta*
for five pesos.
Racing your bike down an alley
with your headphones on
(which is neither safe nor allowed)
but paying attention so
you are in the right place at the right time
to notice the bird, trapped and,
for all it knows,
doomed.
Spanish still requires tokens,
something you can hold in your hand.
The bird,
held in your hand
looking at you, you're sure,
until it flies away,
is its own reward.
You've said all you need to say
for now.
You allow me to kiss your
very slightly raspy cheek
and you give my shoulder
the swift, sweet pats
that are your signature caress.
Then you're gone
for the evening, leaving me
honored
by two jubilant
stories spinning,
shimmering
like a single striped top
you've expertly balanced on its point.

Seeing You Whole

(for Steve)

I've longed to tell you this, but I'm afraid
you'll find the story trite, or lacking grace,
or overwrought, the poetry wanting.
I've chosen the sestina as the form
in hopes it might impress you in itself
no matter what the content as a whole.
Here's what's happened: Lately I've been wanting
to learn to give mortality a form—
my death, and yours; the fact of death itself,
which has been making both of us afraid—
to make acquaintance with it straight and whole,
and come to know its metamorphic grace.
It's you, my love, who've held me back, a form
of adoration turning on itself.
I've been afraid to think of you afraid
of everything we'll lose to death, the whole
substance of our everyday state of grace.
I couldn't bear to think of you wanting
me, and me not being here. In the whole
scheme of things, I've been beset by wanting
nothing bad to happen to you. No form
of difficulty at all. The false grace
of life lived easily. I am afraid
that love has taken on a life itself

that's hidden from me your specific grace
and made me less respectful than afraid.
Afraid to love the infinite and whole

space between us that feels like death itself.
In candlelit half-trance I sat, wanting
to call death out of where its shadows form,

but didn't dare because of you. Itself
a dare, I said aloud the bitter whole
of it: "I'll watch Steve die," the awful grace,
"or else Steve will watch me die," not wanting
to know this,
feeling a bliss start to form,

not wanting to betray you.
Not afraid.
Suddenly not afraid.
Infinite grace:
"One of us will watch the other die." Whole,
holy, an honor, itself wanting form.

Poem Cycle For Steve: Our House

1. Saying The Pictures

In the brief span between
first word and complex sentence,
the older of our little girls would insist, every time,
"Grandma, say the pictures."
That's become my memory, not hers;
when I invite her that way now, she doesn't know what I
mean.
But still she'll start reciting from the landing:
"That's me, huh? That's you, huh?
That's your dad, he died, huh?"
Plainly she doesn't believe
the round-faced fifth-grader is
her bearded, tattooed daddy,
or her adored Poppy
the skinny kid with wild red hair,
But she wants to hear it all anyway,
every time.
"That's my auntie, huh? That's my uncle,
that's my little cousin one time she ate a bee, huh?
That's me."
Saying the pictures,
securing her place
in the gallery of
our house.

2, Certain Light

Some falls,
the south-facing Englemann ivy
turns jewel into a verb,
incites me to chant sumptuous words
scarlet and cinnabar, burnt umber, vermilion,
green.
Light through tall stairway windows, always
a certain light,
dazzles then,
jewels the barred banister
and the finial ball with reflections
spherical and synecdochal,
tints the white cat pink
and my sleep-sallow morning skin
dreamlike iridescent.
This splendor might last
two weeks.

Then, a hard freeze. Overnight,
no color but brown,
no shape but torn and curled
and mostly fallen.
A certain stark incandescent gray
sheens leaded glass.
Wind, sleet.
Squirrels shelter between glass and vine,
surely not much protection now
when they need it.
The cats glower on the windowsill,
tail tips twitching
in faux threat.

I love this about our house:
that squirrels and cats
on either side of a window pane
are safe,
as safe as anyone gets,
in a certain light.

3. Drum

Later I'd realize
I'd heard the noise before,
in another chimney, in
a life part of this one
though I didn't know it then.

Then, as now,
my first thought
to the thrumming through three stories
of interior walls was
ghost.
Wishful thinking or dread?
Or failure of aesthetic nerve,
going for the easy metaphor
instead of simple truth?

A woodpecker, that's what I think,
drumming
on the pipe that lines the chimney.
No bugs there; he's hit upon
how to make more seductive commotion than other males
who'll settle for puny fence posts and utility poles.
Early this year. February.

You say it's wind shaking the pipe. But
in this morning's thirty-mile-an-hour gusts
the windchime is cacophonous,
the chimney pipe

silent.
A handful of arguable explanations, then.
In order of ascending appeal:
wind,
ghost,
woodpecker.
More trouble than it's worth
to prove.
So let it be,
our house with a friendly little
mystery
right through its core.

4. Dancing In The Kitchen

The cleaning lady tells me ours
is the only one of her kitchens
really used.
She means cooked in, dirtied:
bread dough on teal walls,
onion skins scaling yellow counters,
pots boiled over.

High in my arms, the toddler nestles,
shuts her eyes to
LeAnn Rimes and Dvorak from the corner radio
and issues around her thumb
a cozy command:
"Dance."
Hearing aids out,
she might not hear all
the music in our house,
but there's something about
dancing in the kitchen
she
and I
can use.

5. Trying on Clothes

There you sit, patiently
in the barrel chair, limned
by the cream-colored bevel of light
from under the green shade,
feet sturdily on the floor, hands
laced over your belly.

So anxious my throat aches,
I'm trying on clothes.
"How do I look?"
Of course
it's a cliché,
but there's more at stake than that.
My body is
peculiar.
I'm rather fond of it, but
clothes aren't made for it anymore,
and mirrors
when I can see in them at all
blur and halo,
obscure as much as they reveal,
and I can't just stay here
in our house
in T-shirts and jeans.

So it's up to you.
"Nice" tells me nothing.
"Fine" is faint damnation.
"Gorgeous"
is what I'm going for,
though I doubt that would be enough, either.
"Unbelievably beautiful" might work.
"A veritable vision of loveliness."

Finally:
"You look—"
in husbandly desperation—
"pretty."
And I
preen.

6. Disorder

Plants dripping,
dropping leaf litter.
Cats leaving pungent mounds
beside
the litter box.
Into our house
I bring disorder.
Drainage bottles like a litter of fat squirming
gerbils under my shirt.
The endless near-blind litter of
objects I can't find places I can't get to things I can't do
alone.
Our marriage is
a clean, high, supple
litter
transporting me through
my own messes.

The Cello

She even has a name for it
and tells it to me with a smile,
blushing,
a gesture sad and radiant,
for she knows she is beautiful:
"Deading."
"Deading them."
The ones she means
are those who ask too much from her,
wanting,
to talk about important things,
to see her more than she can bear,
liking
her grace, her fluid hands, her wit,
the confidence with which she moves,
thinking,
like me,
too soon, importunate,
that this is someone I could love.
A boy with tattoos on his hands
begins a high riff on a flute,
startling
us both. A woman wearing plaid
bows in white hair drums boogie tunes.
Ceiling
fans whir. It's a former boyfriend
and her mother—needy, left—she's
mourning,
relieved of; it's her oldest friend

who came to want too much.
Not me
slicing
the dark substantial loaf, she gives
a piece to me. I love good bread,
tasting
it in my soul. She shrugs. "I live
without them, cut them off," she says.
"I make them dead to me," a calm
confession and a subtle boast,
shaking,
shaking her head, her hair a sheen
of silver-blonde across her throat
hiding
her mouth. "I don't know how to keep
myself intact except to run.
Running
relaxes me. I know it's mean.
It's awful. When I'm done, I'm done."
Leaning
as far from her as I can get
while in her presence nonetheless,
knowing
that this is not abandonment,
not yet, I don't quite dare to ask.
A cello joins the flute. We sip
lemonade. I understand this
warning,
though I'm not sure she intends it.
I want to say the cello is
praying,
for me always epiphany.
But that might be too intimate,
risking
death. So: "I like the cello." She

smiles. "Me, too. It's my favorite.
Saying
what my boundaries are would mean that
I might have to hurt the person's
feelings."
"And deading them won't hurt them? What?"
"But I won't know it. I'll be gone."
I didn't notice when the flute
Stopped. I'm worried by its absence.
Staring
at where the flautist was, she looks
sad. The drummer's fallen silent.
Soaring,
the cello's song, responsible
to its companion, urges me—
living—
to make myself vulnerable.
"Do you expect someday to be
deading
me? Just so I know." Subterfuge
pointless, she takes time to answer,
telling
the truth. "I swear I'll try not to."
Between us, the cello murmurs.

Woman Wailing

She had the most beautiful hair, black
And glossy as passion, deep and dense,
Thick, heavy as love unrequited.
I'd think of him touching it, hands tense.
It fell to the small of her broad back.
The panes of our windows would rattle,
Transparent before her. She stormed when
Inside it was warm and well-lighted,
But not for her, not for her children.
I saw I'd been pitched into battle.
Listening to her wailing, he'd say,
"I never could have loved her, you know.
My life is with you. It's decided."
I'd swaddle the baby and say, "No.
You'd better make sure she stays away."
I'd try not to think about, later,
That hair streaming over the faces
Of four-year-old Annie and Michael,
Not yet two. Their breath bubbling traces
As she held them under the water.

Cacodemon

What the fuck am I doing here? Kimberly rose
To her knees as the man on the bed moaned and stirred.
There was movement beside him, and Kimberly froze,
But neither the man nor her best friend would have heard,
By the morning, her hand on the latch of the screen,
Her insatiable mouth at his nipples and groin.
They would not tell each other the dizzying dream.
"Yes, I love you," they'd pledge to each other again.
And why am I doing this? Kimberly slithered
In under the covers, in under his skin,
Beneath his malaise where the passion once gathered,
Going down on the spot where the fever had been,
Sucking and swallowing, biting and burrowing,
Flooding her throat and her gut with his energy
Seminal fluid for shooting up. Worrying
Penis and scrotum as if they were liturgy.
By the time she was finished (though not satisfied,
Never once satisfied, finished only in name),
He was hers. He was sick. She withdrew, horrified,
As he hardened in sleep and unconsciously came.
She did not want him. His wife was her oldest friend.
She was visiting him every night. Diseased herself,
Agitated, obsessed, she did not understand.
When he died, it was she whom his wife called for help.
Kimberly had been married for seventeen years
To a man who was safe. Being safe was the goal.
Being settled, predictable, normal, and clear.

Being whole, or allowing the pretense of whole.

Every March 6 and June 3 she'd visit the graves
Of her parents, not so much to mourn as to rave
And demand explanations. *How could you? And how
Could I let you?* Her husband would rescue her there,
Take her home to the safety he'd made for her now,
And she'd let him.
But then came the nightly despair
She could hardly identify, could not contain.
What possessed me? Fleeing. Invading the bed
And the dreams and the bones of a woman or man
She had met on the bus, at the store, on the Net,
In the park, in the graveyard. They couldn't resist,
Or didn't. They'd give her a sign, and she'd follow.
She would straddle them, settle her weight on their chests,
And kiss them and probe them until they were hollow,
Though she was not filled. Never filled. Never sated.
Never able to sleep through the night.
"Kimberly.
Please, Kim, I adore you!" her husband berated.
Knowing only he'd lost her, was losing her, he
Took her into his arms and would not let her go.
"No!" She loved him. She struggled and made her escape
To the cemetery. He went after her, though
He knew he shouldn't.
She surrendered. On the graves
Of her parents, she mounted him, pinned his arms, crushed
Her desperate mouth to his mouth, forced it open,
Took everything in him, and more. He was hers. Hushed
And empty, she cradled him. *What have I done?*

ABOUT THE AUTHOR

Melanie Tem passed away Feb 9, 2015. She was a writer, an oral storyteller, a teacher, a social worker, a wife, a mother, and a grandmother. She received the Bram Stoker, International Horror Guild, British Fantasy, and World Fantasy Awards for her writing, which included almost a hundred short stories, twelve solo novels, and numerous plays, poems, and storytelling performances. Among her novels: *Prodigal, Wilding, Revenant, The Yellow Wood*, and *Black River*, a fictional exploration of grief as a hero's journey. As a social worker and administrator, she worked for the elderly, the disabled, and adoptive children and parents. Her speech on unconditional commitment is still used in parts of the country in the training of prospective adoptive parents.

Curious about other Crossroad Press books?
Stop by our site:
http://store.crossroadpress.com
We offer quality writing
in digital, audio, and print formats.